Make Peace with Your Harshest Critic: You

*How to Break the Habit of
Destructive Self-Talk*

BY GRAHAME COSSUM

MAKE PEACE WITH YOUR HARSHEST CRITIC: YOU

(How to Break the Habit of Destructive Self-Talk)

BY GRAHAME COSSUM

Cossum Publications , 72B Sheskin Road, Greysteel , Co. Derry/ Londonderry, Northern Ireland, BT473BH
http://www.innercritic.net, info@innercritic.net

This book is dedicated to my beloved, loving,

and long-suffering wife, Myfanwy

Acknowledgements

I would like to thank my long-suffering wife, Myfanwy. She had to endure my endless writing and rewriting plus twenty years of hearing me talk about the mind.

I would like to thank my mother and father for their unswerving support and holding my hand when I needed it.

I would like to thank in equal parts those people who knew I would write this book, and those who thought I wouldn't. You each inspired me in your own particular way.

About the Author

Grahame Cossum is a certified Clinical Hypnotherpist, and a Neurolinguistic Programming practitioner. He is also an Integral Eye Movement practitioner, and has created his own unique style of Behaviour Change Coaching. Most importantly he is a lifelong student of the human mind.

Grahame lives with his wife, Myfanwy, in Northern Ireland, where he divides his free time between archery and target practice, his horses and chickens, and eating chocolate biscuits.

Table of Contents

Acknowledgements.. 4

About the Author... 5

Introduction.. 9

CHAPTER 1 12

   Know Your Enemy 12

CHAPTER 2 16

   So, Who Are You?.. 16

CHAPTER 3 23

   Why You Always Think the Worst........................ 23

CHAPTER 4 29

   Are You Premeditating Failure?............................ 29

CHAPTER 5 37

   When Did Your But Get So Big? 37

CHAPTER 6 44

   Are You Good Enough? 44

CHAPTER 7 51

   'Acceptance' Isn't a Four-Letter Word................. 51

CHAPTER 8 62

   Expectation... 62

CHAPTER 9 67

   The Awareness Solution Technique....................... 67

CHAPTER 10 74

Acknowledge Small Steps of Courage.................74

CHAPTER 11 78

Ten Ways to Change Your Behaviour 78

CHAPTER 12 89

Going for a Goal..89

CHAPTER 13 99

Changing Someone Else's Behaviour 99

CHAPTER 14 106

I Should, You Should 106

CHAPTER 15 112

Worrying About What Others Think 112

CHAPTER 16 124

Believe in Yourself...124

CHAPTER 17 135

Mistakes Are There to Be Made.......................135

CHAPTER 18 142

Perfectionism in an Imperfect World 142

CHAPTER 19 152

Guilt 152

CHAPTER 20 156

Who Said Life Was Fair? 156

CHAPTER 21 162

  Feeling Pissed Off Is Okay................................. 162

CHAPTER 22 166

  Mind Your Language, You Loser 166

CHAPTER 23 172

  Confidence Is Simple, Not Easy 172

CHAPTER 24 183

  Be True to Yourself When You Can 183

CHAPTER 25 189

  'No'— A Short Sentence to Use Often 189

CHAPTER 26 196

  Final Thoughts... 196

Introduction

Does it feel at times that your mind has been hijacked by an unseen enemy? An enemy who seems to enjoy playing with your emotions and keeping you well within your comfort zone? An enemy who enjoys telling you, "You are not good enough"?

Excellent, you belong to a club which currently boasts seven billion members. Although by the time I finish this book, it will probably be closer to ten billion. Not feeling good enough is a characteristic shared by everyone on the planet. Why this is so will become obvious as you read through each chapter. This is not a typical self-help book. It's more of a help-yourself voyage of self-awareness.

➢ **For now, all you need to know is that you are not alone.**

Sometimes in life an unexpected event occurs which affects us in a devastating and far-reaching way. One of those events happened to me.

I had a serious horse-riding accident fifteen years ago, the sort of accident that if described to you, it would make you cringe. I will spare you the details. The accident resulted in me losing the three jobs I was

9

holding down, as well as all the hobbies I loved. My friends deserted me when I needed them most. As if that weren't bad enough, as a result of the accident I suffered ten years of depression and nearly lost my mind.

My inner critic was an unseen enemy who delighted in torturing me on a daily basis; I wore "you're not good enough" like a coat. I was desperate to crawl out from underneath this boulder which was crushing the life out of me … and I did.

> **I found a way to make peace with my inner critic, and I am going to share it with you.**

Let me tell you how effective what you are about to learn can be. During my journey through ten years of depression, I became fascinated with the human mind. I decided I wanted to help others in my position to realise *their* full potential.

Three years of training followed which resulted in me becoming a Clinical Hypnotherapist, a Neurolinguistic Programming practitioner, and an Integral Eye Movement practitioner. I even created my own unique style of Behaviour Change Coaching, which I will be using throughout the book. I was good to go and ready to help the world, or so I thought. I opened my business just before the worldwide recession hit .You can guess what happened next.

The recession killed my business, dug a deep hole, buried it, and just for good measure, threw the shovel in as well, all within two years.

Here's the interesting thing: I had trained my reactions to my inner critic to such an extent that I was able to dust myself down and move on with the next chapter of my life, which is the book you are now holding. There were no recriminations, no feelings of "I'm not good enough." I'm going to show you how to react the same way.

I designed this book to enable you to think about your own personal situation in a completely new light. It will let you see that you are actually good enough. It's just that sometimes you can't see the woods for the trees, so to speak.

> **I will supply you with your very own mind machete, so you can hack your way out of the tangled mess.**

I don't have a PhD in psychology—which is a good thing; you won't have to look through a thesaurus to understand what I'm talking about. What I do have, however, is experience: fifteen years of experience on how the inner critic can devastate a life. I have in-depth knowledge of how to react to the inner voice, which I am going to share with you. This isn't a book based on theories that don't work out in the real world. I have personally lived every page in my own life. So if you are ready to take a journey with someone who understands what it is like to have your own voice tell you, "You're not good enough," just turn the page.

CHAPTER 1

Know Your Enemy

Your inner critic is not really your enemy. It's as much a part of you as your breathing. If you think of your inner voice as your enemy, it means you have to go into battle to defeat it. This is a battle that's impossible to win because you will be fighting yourself, and you can't fight what you are. Understanding *how* your inner critic works is the key to making peace with it, and, in turn, making peace with yourself.

The reason the inner critic gets so much bad press is easy to understand. It seems to keep us scared and well within our comfort zone. It also seems to always take a negative point of view on every thought we have. It does these things for a very good reason. The inner critic serves two vital roles:

- It keeps us safe by keeping things the same.

- It gives us an alternative perspective on any thought we have.

The inner critic cannot be switched off, as it is a hardwired evolutionary program that is designed to protect you. We don't need to switch it off; what we need is a different way of responding to the stream of negative chatter we experience on a daily basis. Later I will give you details of how and why your inner voice came to exist, but for now just accept it does exist for you, me, and everyone else on the planet.

It would be very easy for me to now say, "Ignore the voice and get on with living." The fact is, your inner voice won't be ignored. It will always find a way to make itself heard, regardless of how much you try to do the opposite. "Ignore the voice and get on with it" is simplistic advice, and doomed to failure. There is no single answer to making peace with your inner critic. A combination of understanding and accepting how it works are the keys to transforming your reactions to it.

For instance, when the internal critic says "That's not good enough" or "You messed up," it's not the words themselves that cause the problems, it's the *meaning* we attach to them. We take the words and embellish them. (Later I will show you how to identify those times when we give meaning where no meaning actually exists.)

For instance, when we hear "That's not good enough," we may think "I'm not good enough." When the inner critic says, "You messed up," we might turn that into "I always fail. I'm no good." It seems like the inner critic is just giving us a hard time, but it's actually providing useful information and feedback.

13

The problem is the meaning or interpretation we give to that internal voice. We victimise ourselves with our own self-damaging thoughts. It's not the inner critic saying you're not good enough; it's you telling yourself you're not good enough.

Recognising you are potentially victimising yourself is a very important concept to understand, and it will come up again throughout this book. I'll help release you from this mind trap, if you're willing to take the small steps required to awaken the courage you have always had.

In the following chapters, we will explore areas of life where we experience the inner critic at work— areas such as making mistakes, perfectionism, acceptance, and worrying about what other people think of you. I will then show you a different way to respond to your inner voice—a way that is quick and effective.

Sometimes it can be unnerving to learn a new skill, but rest assured the results you achieve will be worth the effort. It can be uncomfortable reflecting on certain areas of your life. It can make us feel uneasy to admit to realities we would rather not admit to. That's okay. You are human after all, not a machine. The good news is it doesn't take very long to adapt to a new way of thinking. Trust yourself long enough to uncover your courage.

You want to make peace with the inner critic, so you can make peace with yourself. *Nothing* is more important. A vital part of the jigsaw is understanding yourself, so let's find out who you are and why you do what you do.

CHAPTER 2

So, Who Are You?

I understand this particular question can be quite difficult to answer, as sometimes we feel as if we are someone else. At times we feel we are not in control and we just seem to react to whatever life throws our way. Sometimes it can be scary just being ourselves. We say we are going to do something, and then do the complete opposite. We say we are going to make changes in our lives and then don't take any action. Other times we just seem to be waiting for someone or something to show up and rescue us. I know exactly how you feel, as I have been there myself.

Here's the good news: you are a work in progress. It is completely natural and normal to be and do all of those things. Being a contradiction is part of being human. We only run into problems when we think such tendencies are not normal and try to fight them, and when we do so, we end up fighting with ourselves. We can certainly change and adapt how we react to our inbuilt tendencies; it is how we do it that creates the problems. Waging a war on yourself is never a good idea.

Let me give you an example of what I mean. Have you ever beaten yourself up and called yourself weak because you wanted to make a change in your life but it never got past the thinking stage? Me, too. I was once given the opportunity to build a house in a perfect location. What did I do? I turned the opportunity down flat, despite the fact it was what I wanted. I was listening too closely to my inner critic; fear of the unknown and self-contradiction were keeping me from my dream. Fortunately on this occasion, no harm was done, as my wife had an alternative view on my fear. She persuaded (which is secret code for "bullied") me to take a leap of faith and go for it. The house was built, and we all lived happily ever after. (She made me write that bit).

Let me walk you through a few examples of how we all live contradictions in our lives:

- We say we want to lose weight, but continue to eat junk food.

- We say we want to get fit, so we join a gym and never go.

- We want to meet people, but never socialise.

- We eat chocolate biscuits when we know they are bad for us. Hold on, that was about me. Let's ignore that last bit.

I would like you to understand that the information I am giving you can never be a complete picture, as we are unique individuals. When we talk about human beings there will *always* be exceptions to the rule. So keeping this in mind, let's explore *why* we do what we do.

You are a living, breathing contradiction driven by emotions and feelings. Your evolution continues to play a major role in shaping who you are. The fact that you utter the words "I'm not good enough" has more to do with your evolutionary survival than a judgement of you as a person. Here is the reason.

You have a conscious, logical mind and a subconscious, analogical mind. The conscious mind allows you to process and make sense of the data in front of you, such as the squiggles and symbols on this page. It weighs, considers, and plans. The subconscious mind does everything else, processing up to four million pieces of information per second.

The subconscious doesn't care much what your conscious mind thinks as it is in the driving seat. It is regulating your temperature and blood flow, even your breathing, and does all this outside of your conscious awareness.

The subconscious has another vital role: it keeps you safe. It does this by keeping things the same as they have always been, and will resist any attempt by the conscious mind to change what you are currently doing. *Unless you know how to work with it. And you will after you have finished this book.*

So, why are we a contradiction when we know, logically, what is supposed to be good for us?

The clue is in the word "logical". We are driven by the subconscious, non-logical part of the mind, which likes everything to stay the same. This explains why you eat at the same times, even if you're not hungry. It's why you dress in a particular order and even put your shoes on in the same way. The list is endless.

The subconscious mind learns by repetition and turns repeated behaviour into a habit. It also will resist every attempt to change the habit, unless you know how to work with it. The techniques and strategies you'll learn here are simple to use and quick to implement, but they require repetition and a will to change. I'll now give you a quick demonstration of how your subconscious mind and your inner critic resist change.

> **What follows is an exercise which is quite difficult and will take some time to complete. It requires a notepad and pen.**

Resist turning the page and think about the last sentence for thirty seconds.

Did you feel it? Did you experience your subconscious mind and inner critic resisting? Even as you read the sentence, a little voice inside your head was probably saying, "Sounds like hard work," "I don't have the time," or "Maybe I will get back to the book when my head is in the right place."

Did you feel the resistance to my suggestion? I just triggered something in your subconscious mind that lies innate within all of us. As a species, we have an inbuilt program which dictates that anything perceived as *difficult* has the potential to move us away from pleasure and towards pain.

You have just experienced a demonstration of how your inner critic works. It resisted your attempt at potentially upsetting the status quo. It doesn't want things to change. It wants you to stay exactly the way you are.

Our minds are constantly assessing whether we are moving toward pleasure or pain. I am sure you can guess which your mind prefers the most. My use of the word *difficult* was intentional. I wanted your subconscious mind to register that it was just about to do something painful, psychologically speaking.

Some of you may be thinking, "No that's not it. I was just feeling lazy." Well, that's how your mind communicates with you when it doesn't want to waste precious resources moving toward something it perceives as painful. It communicates with you in a variety of subtle ways: "I procrastinate," "I couldn't be bothered," or "I know I should, but ..." are just some of the things you have maybe heard yourself saying.

Recognising this is completely normal allows you to become aware of what your automatic reactions to perceived difficulty are. Once we are aware, we can make different choices regarding those reactions.

Of course, being human, there is always another option. You might well be actually just lazy, in which case if you wrap some towels around this book it makes an excellent pillow. I will prod you with a sharp stick when we get to the next chapter.

Remember this little demo as you go through the book, and I will share with you how to recognise this automatic reaction and change it.

Before we go any further, I have a confession to make. I absolutely loathe seeing exercises in a self-help book which require the insight and patience of a Buddhist monk to complete. It reminds me too much of being back at school and having to do homework. I have decided to make a complete departure from the norm and *not* give you exercises that require a ream of paper and a dozen pens to do (can you tell I am over thirty?) I am not your headmaster/mistress, and you are not my pupil. We are just two people on a journey. The only difference between us is I brought a map for us to follow.

There are plenty of thinking processes in the following chapters. There will be plenty of aha moments and moments of self-awareness. Naturally there will also be plenty of solutions. You might laugh, you might cry, you might want to pull the pages out with your teeth. I will help you challenge yourself, so you may grow beyond your current limitations and fears. You *could* use a scrap of paper for scribbling notes, if you so desire, but it is not an absolute requirement. Or you could do what I do: write in the margins and ruin the book.

That's the technical stuff out of the way. I could go into a lot more detail about neurons and neural pathways, which would be about as interesting as listening to grass grow, and won't help your understanding of the process one little bit. So, if you are ready to hit the road together, then let's go.

CHAPTER 3

Why You Always Think the Worst

You know the feeling. The phone rings in the middle of the night. Your chest tightens and your heart beats faster, as you brace yourself for what must be bad news. Your hand reaches slowly for the phone as your mind races with thoughts of impending doom.

You say hello, not really wanting the caller to answer. Then the caller says hello and pauses, only adding to the increasing tension. At last the caller speaks, "I am calling to see if you would be interested in buying insurance." You breathe a massive sigh of relief, and then want to throttle him.

Let's find out *why* we always think the worst, and why it is completely normal. Is it because you always see the negative side of life? No. Is it because life never goes as planned? No.

We could go at this for the next few hours, and the answer would still be no. Until by some miracle we stumbled over the correct answer: Is it because the job of the subconscious mind and the inner critic is to place you on alert, if something happens out of the norm, like a midnight phone call, for instance? Yes.

I think of all the common attributes we share, always thinking the worst is probably the most annoying and the least understood. Understanding why you think the worst is of vital importance, as once you understand what is happening you can accept it as just another part of the human experience, while stepping out of the grip this kind of thinking holds.

Let me take you through a short story of our ancestors from thousands of generations ago. It will help you see why we have a tendency to look on the dark side. All human beings come with an in-built danger radar for detecting potential threats—a radar that was of vital importance to our ancestors. Anything out of the ordinary was a potential life-or-death situation for them. Was that bush moving because of the wind, or could it be a sabre-toothed tiger looking to make a tasty breakfast out of me? Either way, it doesn't matter to the radar. The suspect situation activates the brain's fight-or- flight mechanism and prepares your body to either fight or run—by releasing adrenaline into the bloodstream … just in case.

Now spin forward a few thousand generations to the present day. You still have the in-built radar and also the fight-or-flight mechanism. It still gets activated when something happens out of the normal course of everyday events. The midnight phone call is not normal, so you are triggered into survival mode. We can't actually switch this survival mode off. We can, however, modify our reaction to it, which I will explain later.

For now I want you to have a thirty-second think. When have you thought the worst and nothing happened? I'll give you an example of my own, by way of illustration.

I vividly remember the last time I was on holiday, when I was coming through the customs checkpoint. I was in the *nothing to declare line* when a customs officer gave me that look. You know the one. It makes you feel like you're standing with a neon sign on your head that says "criminal." My heart started beating faster. I wasn't even carrying any duty-free items, but I felt like I was smuggling contraband into the country. Visions of me standing naked in a prison cell getting strip-searched, raced through my mind. The relief I felt when I cleared customs was immense. I felt like I had pulled off the crime of the century, but why? I hadn't done anything!

My brain had been hijacked by the same primitive program that kept my ancestors alive all those thousands of years ago, and I was powerless to resist. My radar had detected something out of the norm and reacted accordingly. Understanding what is happening inside your mind is the first step to reacting in a different way.

Although at times it can be a real pain, the fight-or-flight mechanism is there to protect you. If it weren't there, every thought you had would seem logical, like it was the right thing to do. For instance:

25

- I think I will put my hand in the fire ... yeah, why not?

- I think I will drive the car at 140 mph ... sounds good.

- I think I will jump off a tall building ... ought to be fun.

Imagine life without the protection mechanism. Actually, you don't have to imagine it, since without it, you would be dead. It's normal, it's natural, and it's part of who we are. It can't be switched off unless the part of the brain that controls the mechanism is damaged.

There's a downside to always thinking the worst. Take it from me, a former world-class expert. (I was so bad my own mother used to say I worried about having nothing to worry about.) While it's natural to have worst-scenario thoughts, getting stuck in them— believing in them—is a habit you want to break. The potential side-effects of getting stuck in worry are anxiety, frustration, and in extreme cases even depression. When we dwell on worse-case scenarios, we start to attach meaning to our negative thought patterns, for instance:

- If I'm thinking "I'm not good enough", then I'm not.

- If I'm thinking "I'm selfish," then I must be.

Can you see how much harm can be done with this train of thought? It doesn't end there. This train of thought can easily become a belief about ourselves that we accept as true. If it remains unchallenged, our mind will do what it does naturally: it will look to the outside world for evidence to support the belief.

Let me ask you a question. Have you ever noticed when you think about buying a car, the roads seem to be filled with the same car in the exact same colour? This phenomenon is called *priming*. Put simply: If you think about something often enough, you will start to notice it in your environment, and pay more attention to it.

Can you see how priming has the potential to make you feel not good enough or selfish if you are priming yourself to look for evidence to this effect?

Can we avoid thinking the worst, or at least tone it down a bit? Let me share a simple technique to employ when you're caught in this mind trap. You challenge your own thoughts by taking a step back, counting to ten, and asking:

> ➤ **Is what I am thinking actually true?**

Nine times out of ten, it isn't. It's just your mind's attempt at keeping you safe. If it is true—well, at least now you have information to work with. If it isn't true, it's time to accept the thought for what it was—just another meaningless, random thought—and move on. This technique is so simple, yet so effective. It stops automatic "thinking the worst" thoughts dead in their tracks. I wish I had known this technique when coming through the customs hall. I might have spared myself the images of rubber gloves and guys in white coats.

We can train ourselves out of the "thinking the worst" style of thinking. It takes time and effort, but the results can be spectacular. I would highly recommend giving this technique a good trial in daily life. It has certainly helped me and my clients on hundreds of occasions. I am confident it will also help you.

> **Helpful hint: Be an observer of your thoughts, not a referee.**

CHAPTER 4

Are You Premeditating Failure?

I have decided to give you a break, so go put the kettle on and make yourself a nice cup of coffee. While you are there, can I have a cup of tea? What! You have no tea? I suppose coffee will have to do.

Have you ever wondered why sometimes, despite our best intentions, we get stuck for no apparent reason? We then start beating ourselves up because we feel we have no willpower or we aren't good enough. When actually, any intention can fall foul of the mental process you *have* to go through before it becomes a reality.

Well, sit back, put your feet up, and enjoy the next ten minutes.

Premeditating failure: what does it mean? Have you got it? How do you recognise it? Don't worry, it isn't a heart condition. It's more of a mind condition, which you can treat yourself if you know what to look for.

How many times in your life have you set out with good intentions to do something, only to talk yourself out of it before you have even started? Well, you are not alone. We all have had that experience. Hence the saying, "The road to hell is paved with good intentions." So why do we do that? Are we not logical-thinking humans?

Evolution has devised a cunning little mind game we have to play before it lets us run headfirst into something it perceives as having the potential for danger. We have an inbuilt protection mechanism that is activated when we either want to change something we are currently doing or even just think about it. The mechanism is there to protect you from yourself. It's a pain, I know, but it's there nonetheless.

This mechanism will resist any attempt at change unless you know how it works and how to work with it. So now that you know why the mechanism is there and what it does, we will go into the "how" of making changes without making alarm bells ring.

There are four distinct levels your mind *has* to pass through before it will allow changes to be made:

- Rejection

- Confusion

- Understanding

- Clarity

I will explain the four levels in detail in a moment, but just realising they are there puts you at a major advantage. It will help you understand what is going on in your mind when you decide, for instance, to change your job or change something in your life.

As a little experiment, take sixty seconds—right now—and think about changing something major in your life. Pick something that might be nice to change, then make sure you take a full sixty seconds to really think about it. Contemplate what it would be like for you if you made this change.

Go ahead. I'm waiting!

[Time out for churning mental processes ...]

There. So what happened? Maybe initially you felt a little excitement, but I can guarantee that within a few seconds you started asking yourself "what if" questions. What if this bad thing happened? Or that bad thing? That's your protection mechanism at work. Either that, or I'm a mind reader.

Here are the four levels explained:

- **Rejection** – This is when an idea is rejected out of hand before you have had time to even think about it. You will do this the vast majority of the time because you have just activated a very primitive part of your brain, which is responsible for "fight or flight." At this level, your brain is telling you to run away from potential danger. It might be only a thought of change, but it's something new, and this part of your brain is now on high alert. This explains those times when someone has suggested something even slightly out of your comfort zone, and you rejected it out of hand but did not understand why.

- **Confusion** – At this level you have moved on from rejection mode, but now you have two conflicting thoughts trying to occupy the same space. The inner conversation will sound like, "I want to, but I don't know how," or maybe, "I'm not good enough/attractive enough/smart enough to do that." Unfortunately, most people will get stuck at this level and go no further because they are listening to those thoughts and accepting them as real, not realising they are in the middle of a process which has another two steps.

- **Understanding** – This is when you have passed through the first two levels and will start to formulate a plan to get whatever it is you want to achieve. Once you get to this level, the mind will switch from stopping you to helping you. This is when you get ideas and insights, but you have to get there first.

- **Clarity** – Congratulations! If you have reached this stage, you know exactly what to do, when to do it, and how long it is going to take. You are not worried that all the information you need isn't available, as you know it will come to you. Potentially, you could revisit any of the other stages for a short period, but you are confident about what you want.

There is no shortcutting this process for getting yourself to change: it is hardwired into you by evolution. There could be other variables included, but basically the structure remains the same.

At this point, I would like to make a suggestion: why not write those four levels down on a sheet of paper or place them in a memo on your phone—anywhere prominent where you will see them on a regular basis?

Look at them when you have a decision to make or want to make a change, and you will be able to identify immediately which level you are at. If you're finding resistance to making changes in your life or finding it difficult to make a decision, then realise you are somewhere between levels one and two. This is your mind's way of telling you it needs more information in order to proceed to the understanding level.

If you find you have trouble making *any* kind of decision, then curiously enough, decision-making isn't your problem (after all, you decided to buy this book). Taking responsibility for the consequences that flow from your decision is the problem, as it will always be easier to blame someone or something for a negative outcome than to take full responsibility yourself.

If this is the case, use this chapter in combination with the next chapter,

"When Did Your But Get So Big?" Together they should give you an insight into why you are doing what you are doing, or rather not doing.

Let me give you an example of the four levels at work, from a personal perspective:

- **Me**: I think I will write a book.

  My mind: Don't be daft. Who do you think you are? You're not good enough. You have nothing interesting to say. (*rejection*)

- **Me**: I am between levels one and two, so I will ignore the ranting of my internal voice and push on.

  My mind: How many chapters? How long will it take? How will you get it published? Who will edit it for you? (*confusion*)

- **Me**: My job is to write, not project into a future which hasn't happened. I will cross those bridges as I come to them.

  My mind: Let's have a look at what is currently out there and do something different. (*understanding*)

- **Me**: I will write a chapter a week. It will take about one year. I can always enlist the help of a freelance editor and proof-reader. (*clarity*)

This is obviously a very condensed version of what actually happened when I decided to write this book, but you get the idea. The whole point of this process—actually the whole point of the book—is to enable you to be become aware of your own internal processes, and in doing so become content with who and what you are, and with what is going on inside your own mind.

Once you become aware of your own internal processes, you will quickly notice that people around you seem to be in a self-induced sleepwalk. They seem to be waiting for the perfect version of themselves to show up, the version that isn't depressed, isn't angry, and is always happy. They will all have one thing in common: they moan a lot about how bad their life is, but do absolutely nothing about it.

If you lend them this book, don't expect to get it back as they are "going to read it next week." They will still be reading it "next week" a year from now. Sad but true.

Unfortunately, the perfect version of them isn't going to show up any time soon, as they are permanently stuck between levels one and two, waiting for someone or something to come and rescue them. You now have your very own rescue plan. Use it when you feel you are getting stuck.

Here's a thought process for you to do. It might help you understand why in the past you seemed to make an illogical decision about something, but didn't know why. Think about the four levels: rejection, confusion, understanding, and clarity. Now think about an idea you had in the past but did not follow through with. You will probably find you got stranded somewhere between levels one and two. You listened to the ranting of your internal voice and believed what you heard to be true.

Think of a time when you did follow through with an idea and then compare the two. Was there a difference? Can you remember the difference? When you know what you did in the past to turn an idea into a reality, then you can easily transfer this ability onto your new idea which initially seemed impossible. Just keep the four steps in mind as you do this.

Let's get real here for a moment. There will be times an idea will remain just that—an idea—as some things are just not doable, like holding your breath for an hour (if you can hold your breath for an hour and are still alive, I apologise). This process is not designed to help you do the impossible; it is designed to help you identify the reasons for dropping a good idea about making changes in your life because of fear or lack of knowledge. It will help you identify the level you were stuck at, and prevent you from making the same mistake again and again.

I know, I know—I lied when I said I wasn't going to give you a challenge. The real reason I gave you a challenge is because I had to drink your coffee. Maybe next time you will have some tea bags.

CHAPTER 5

When Did Your But Get So Big?

Instead of concentrating on the inner critic, we are instead going to explore its introverted cousin called *cognitive dissonance*. The inner voice of cognitive dissonance is soft and subtle, but it can hold you back very easily. It's the tiny voice that gives you a plausible excuse to continue a behaviour that is detrimental to you. This tiny voice tells you, "It's okay to smoke; it helps with your stress," or maybe "Clean your plate just like you were taught; you shouldn't waste food."

There is no criticism, no making you feel bad, just a little voice telling you, "What you are doing is just fine." My barely audible voice kept me sixty pounds overweight for longer than I care to admit. It was telling me, "It's okay to overeat, that's what depressed people do. And besides, you can't exercise anyhow." It gave me a plausible excuse to maintain a behaviour that was doing me harm. It very effectively removed the option of choice from me, and it's probably doing the same to you.

The good news is, if you can identify where you are using cognitive dissonance to keep a behaviour in place, then the behaviour is easily stopped with a bit of effort on your behalf. The bad news is, if cognitive dissonance isn't confronted and dealt with, then a detrimental behaviour can stay in place for an awfully long time.

> **The real power of the technique for removing cognitive dissonance is the knowledge it will give you. Take this knowledge and use it to make better choices.**

The technique will bring something which is currently in the subconscious mind into conscious awareness. When we become aware of cognitive dissonance, then we can do something about it, rather than letting it do untold harm in the background. This process will transform your life if you master it; it only requires two small steps:

> **Identify where you are using an excuse to maintain a behaviour.**

> **Use the knowledge to change the behaviour.**

So what exactly is cognitive dissonance? It's a psychological term which is used instead of the word "excuse." This excuse allows the mind to keep a behaviour in place, even when you know it's to your detriment. It allows two conflicting thoughts to live in relative harmony so you can maintain a behaviour without feeling guilt or anguish.

So now that you know what it is, how does it concern you? This is where your big but comes in, and I will now give you a few examples to illustrate just how big your but is (okay, no more ass jokes):

- I would like to lose weight, BUT I was taught not to waste food.

- I would like to stop smoking, BUT it helps my stress, and I'm addicted.

- I would like to do xyz, BUT I don't have the time.

- I would like to do all the exercises in this book, BUT they probably only work for other people.

We will be returning to the list later. Can you see a pattern there? Maybe you even recognise yourself in one or two of the examples. That's good, because we all do exactly the same thing. The word "but" effectively removes choice from the equation. You tell yourself that something or someone outside of you is the cause of your problems. You place yourself outside of the problem and assume the role of powerless observer.

I won't pretend there aren't times when you are a powerless observer. Disease, accidents, tragedies, assault, and abuse are a few of those times when choice has been taken away from you, and I don't doubt for a second you do experience real suffering. But in this chapter, we're are talking about those other times— when you have kept a behaviour in place without realising how the mind was playing its part and holding you back.

Let's now return to the list and add the element of choice. These are the choices you are making when you keep a detrimental behaviour in place. They are subconscious choices, but *your* choices nonetheless:

- I would like to lose weight, but I was taught not to waste food. *I am choosing to risk diabetes, heart disease, and stroke rather than waste food.*

- I would like to stop smoking, but it helps with my stress, and I'm addicted. *I am choosing to risk cancer and die early rather than experience stress.*

- I would like to do xyz, but I don't have the time. *I am choosing to do nothing rather than miss my TV programmes or get out of bed an hour earlier.*

- I would like to do all the exercises in this book, but they probably only work for other people. *I am choosing to bury my head in the sand rather than face harsh reality, because that's easier.*

The list is endless. We could go at this for the rest of the book. There are as many instances of cognitive dissonance as there are people on the planet—in fact, many more instances than that, since almost every human being harbours a multiple number of these quiet self-contradictions.

Before we proceed, I would like you to ponder this. Say a person is addicted to smoking or eating sugary foods, and they are diagnosed with some sort of life-threatening illness. Suppose they suddenly stop smoking or stop overeating. Where did the addiction go? Were they using the word "addiction" in another expression of cognitive dissonance? I think it is possible, but I will leave you to think that one through for yourself.

So now let's talk about the technique: how to free yourself from cognitive dissonance. The process that follows is actually quite simple to do. All it requires is about two minutes of your time and a willingness to be completely honest with your answers. Think of something you would like to start or stop. It may help if you scribble it down on a piece of paper, rather than mentally trying to answer these three questions at once.

- I would like to start … BUT_____

Or

- I would like to stop … BUT_____

And

- Instead I am choosing to…_____

Now check and see if you are using cognitive dissonance (an excuse) to keep the behaviour in place, or if there is an actual valid reason you can't stop or start whatever it is you want or don't want to do. Better still, ask someone to give you feedback to ensure you are not just using another excuse.

41

Okay, now you have uncovered some of the subconscious choices you have been making, so now what? I think it would be easier to give you an example from my own life by way of illustration.

When I was at my worst with depression, I had a friend who used to call me every day. He never inquired how I was doing. No, he just wanted to dump his problems on to me. I was in no fit state to listen, but listen I did for longer than I care to admit. I was getting tangled up in his drama, and it was causing me harm.

Despite me telling this friend the problems he was causing, he still persisted. The subconscious choice I was making was to allow this person to stay in my life, regardless of the cost to me or my mental state. I didn't realise then that I was keeping this person in my life because I was scared of offending him. I was worried what he might think of me. Something had to give, and unless I acted, that something was going to be me. Suffice to say this person was removed from my life for the sake of my mental health. Was it easy? No. Did I feel bad about it? Yes. And I won't pretend some of the choices you might be forced to make will be easy. Unfortunately, sometimes hard choices have to be made. That's just part of the human experience.

Tackling cognitive dissonance in your life can be tricky, as it means you have to admit to using an excuse to maintain a behaviour all this time. Nobody likes admitting they were wrong, but if you can get past this hang-up, the results you achieve can be well worth the effort.

You may already be feeling a little bit uncomfortable with this section, but ask yourself this: do I want to acknowledge my problem or do I want to be a victim of it? This is a very powerful process, and you might well be shocked by some of the subconscious choices you are making. The important thing is to start making different choices and not just think about doing it. You will reap the benefits of putting a bit of time and effort into this.

As you go through this process, don't be surprised if you receive a little message from your inner voice saying something like "You are the exception" or "It's not that bad." Just know it's your inner critic trying to keep things the same. It's not reality.

Enjoy the process, and use the knowledge you discover to make changes to your life. It might be smart to revisit this process in the future, if you think you could be using an excuse to maintain some other detrimental behaviour. It's a great way of finding out.

CHAPTER 6

Are You Good Enough?

No, you're not, and you never will be. But keep reading. It's not as bad as it sounds.

What do you share with every other person on the planet? Not your height, not your weight, not your political opinions. It's the feeling that you're not good enough.

Everyone you know as well as everyone you don't know at some time suffers from feelings of not being good enough. It's in our genes. It's there to ensure survival of the species. (I'll explain how in a minute.)

It doesn't matter how intelligent you are or how much money you have. It's the same for everybody. Some people might be able to control it a bit better, but we all still experience it. We need to back up thousands of generations to know why we suffer from feelings of not being good enough.

Human beings are created insatiable. We are hardwired to always want more, to improve our

44

surroundings, to constantly strive to better ourselves. We constantly strive to push the boundaries of everything we come into contact with. If you can imagine back to when we lived in caves, our very survival as a race depended on our being insatiable. We devised quicker and more efficient ways to dispatch what we needed to survive. We lived in small groups, which became larger groups and helped each other, constantly striving to create tools and weapons. This ensured the survival of the human race.

Fast forward to the present day. We still have the same insatiable need to push the boundaries, except today when those needs aren't met we call ourselves failures. We are not good enough, not attractive enough, not rich enough, not happy enough.

Models think they are ugly, anorexics think they are fat, rich people want more money or are scared of losing what they have. Happiness is something only other people possess; at least that's how it looks. We want better cars, better houses, better husbands, better wives, better lives, better everything. And what happens when we don't get all these things? "We are not good enough."

Our evolution has ensured we strive for better and better, and to make sure we keep striving. It also ensures we never reach the end, we are never satisfied, and if we are not satisfied, we must not be good enough. If we are not good enough, we have to try harder ... are you seeing a pattern?

And all this time, you thought it was only you who felt this way. Join the club.

Some of the unhappiest people I have worked with as clients were the very people who outwardly appeared to have everything. Big cars, big houses, big bank accounts, and also big depression.

They felt "not being good enough" more acutely than most. If you think about it, logically it makes perfect sense; they had the most to lose. They would be publically shown to be "not good enough." They normally bounced from anxiety to depression and back again within the same conversation.

Sometimes not feeling good enough expresses as a subtle, almost imperceptible sense of self-doubt. Other times, it's an in-your-face emotion. Parenting must be one of life's areas where "not being good enough" shows up more acutely than possibly anyplace else. Children do not show up with a book of instructions on what to do to make sure they have a happy, successful life filled with wonderful things. Parenting is a learn-as-you-go experience, filled with many mistakes. Is it any wonder you feel confused and frustrated, just like your parents did? Raising kids is a big responsibility to shoulder, and we have to make it up as we go along. So we need to cut ourselves some slack.

I trust you are beginning to see "not being good enough" is not actually your fault. It's no one's fault. It's just part of you. It's part of us like blinking is part of us, and we don't beat ourselves up for blinking, do we?

Even if someone else told you, "You're not good enough," all they did was display a profound ignorance of how the human mind works. They also made the statement based on *their* own internal standards and rules, and unless they showed you a book containing all their rules and standards, then how could you possibly live up to them? Would you even want to? Do you want to live your life to please and impress someone else?

Maybe it's time to let this particular belief about yourself go, now that you can see it for what it is. Some people will have difficulty doing this because they feel victimised by whoever made the statement. If this is you, ask yourself this question, "Do I want to be victimised for the rest of my life by someone who neither knows nor cares what I feel?"

Can you make peace with yourself, or will you continue in the role of victim? Will you take your power back, or will you keep giving it away until all you are left with is a voice that says, "I am no good"?

The fact is you have the power to choose what to do next. You get to choose whether to believe you are no good, or you can choose to believe the complete opposite. I am sure after you have read this complete chapter you will make the right choice based on what you will know.

Are we powerless? Yes and no is the short answer. Yes, we are powerless if our aim is to try and remove an evolutionary program from our subconscious mind. It's just not possible. No, we are not powerless because we can work with this exact same program in a way that puts the power back where it belongs—with us.

The important ingredient in working with the subconscious mind is to never get into an argument with it because, quite simply, you won't win. Your intellect and intelligence don't have the power to dominate something which has evolved over tens of thousands of years. Don't waste your time asking, "*Why* am I not good enough?" as that would be using logic against a part of your mind which is by nature non-logical. Worse still, that part of your mind is not listening.

We need something to answer our inner critic with when it tells us "You're not good enough." Whatever our reply is, it should be something that's easily remembered. It has to be quick and effective, but it also has to work with the subconscious mind in the way *it* was designed to work.

Something along the lines of an affirmation would work perfectly, but here is where you can run into problems. For an affirmation to work, it has to be true. Otherwise, it will be rejected by the subconscious mind and will only further reinforce your sense of not being good enough.

What follows is an antidote to feelings of not being good enough. Although this technique is short, it is extremely powerful. It fulfils all the criteria required to ensure acceptance by the subconscious mind and your inner critic.

When your inner critic is telling you you're not good enough, repeat the following:

> **"I am doing the best I can."**

When we use this affirmation, we are working directly with the subconscious in a way it understands. There are no questions, there are no belief changes required, it's just a statement of fact that is readily accepted. If your inner critic comes back with "Your best is not good enough," then just repeat the affirmation "I am doing the best I can." Your subconscious will eventually get the message. This technique needs to be practiced until it becomes second nature: repetition, repetition, repetition. That is the *only* way to reinforce this message, and to convey it to the subconscious mind.

If your inner critic is telling you "Everything you're reading sounds like hard work," then ask yourself, "How much longer do I want to be a victim of my own thoughts?" It's time to make a choice. When you repeat the affirmation I recommend on a regular basis, you'll find your mind switches from victim mode to solution-finding mode. For this one reason alone, it is a good idea to use it whenever you can.

From a personal perspective, I can say that the affirmation works extremely well in instances where I seem to be locked into a one-track train of thought. It has the ability to clear the fog from my mind, allowing me to think straight. I can't conceive of any area of my life where adopting an attitude of "doing the best I can" has not proven useful. Give it a go on a regular basis, and monitor your results. I think you will be pleased with what you find.

CHAPTER 7

'Acceptance' Isn't a Four-Letter Word

There is a possibility you may already have decided to skip this chapter because you don't want to feel uncomfortable. Reading about acceptance can be uncomfortable, but I would like to ask a little favour of you. Read the following story about a former client of mine, and then make up your mind. It will only take a few minutes of your time.

For the purposes of our story we will call the client "Joe." Joe was a reasonably happy thirty-five year old—recently married, new house, and successfully holding down three jobs. He was a swimming teacher, a personal trainer, and he also worked in his family-run solarium. He had various hobbies, which included bodybuilding and horseback riding.

Little did Joe know, but things were about to take a turn for the worse. To cut a long story short, Joe had a serious accident. Well, actually that's not true. Joe's accident was caused by another person.

He was very lucky not to end up in a wheelchair. He lost his jobs, his hobbies, and also most of his friends. And just for good measure, he suffered depression for years to come. He went from doctor to doctor and specialist to specialist, looking for someone to help him out of the pain he was suffering because of the back injury he now had.

Fast forward to the present day. Joe is no longer depressed. He has the occasional bad day just like everyone else. He is not bitter about the past. He went on to write the book you are now holding in your hand, and hopes after reading to the end of this chapter, you might arrive at a place of acceptance and move on with your life.

That's right. The story is about me, an ordinary person who moved on from something that had devastated my life. If I can do it, so can you.

I'd like to share nine tips that will help you get to acceptance. It may take some effort to apply them, but your effort will be repaid a thousand times over.

1) Change the mindset

What is it about the word "acceptance" that is so highly charged with emotion that it would make you want to throw this book at the wall? Perception is the problem. We perceive acceptance as *giving up* or *giving in.* This goes totally against our hardwired evolution of insatiability and striving.

Even the mere thought of giving up or giving in sets up a conflict in our minds. That's why I am not going to even suggest it. I am not going to tell you that you should "just accept your fate and get on with it." To do so would deny the reality of your situation.

I am, however, going to ask you to get over the belief of what you currently think the word "acceptance" means. Doing so will allow you to move on with your life if you are stuck in the cycle of "Why me?", "Why now?", and "What have I done to deserve this?"

After my accident I seemed to be stuck in a permanent cycle of "Why me?" thoughts. It was driving me insane and draining the life out of me. I was looking to the past and the future for answers which didn't exist, and in doing so I was keeping myself in a permanent state of turmoil.

After a torturous two years, I came to realise that a solution was never going to be found in the past or the future, because I was a human being living very much in the present. The solution had to be found in the here and now.

I overcame the mindset that I was somehow giving up or giving in, when I accepted that *for now* my life had changed and would possibly never be quite the same again. Once I was able to change that mindset, I was able to start digging myself out of the hole where I was being buried alive by my own thoughts.

Notice I didn't change my mindset to "I accept that my life is ruined," or "I accept that I am always going to be miserable." I simply decided to accept that the accident had indeed happened, it had indeed caused certain kinds of damage, and things were indeed different as a result. With this basic acceptance of what had already happened and could not be changed, I created a platform from which I could start to build a new and better life.

2) Keep things real

Every day I made myself come to terms with the way things *actually* were and not how I would like them to be, or how they had been in the past. When I found myself starting to slip into victim mode, with thoughts like "I used to be able to lift three hundred pounds when I did bodybuilding, and now I can barely lift myself out of this chair," or "All of my friends are turncoats who deserted me," I'd hear the thought, then change it to something different: "The accident happened. I have new challenges. My life is different because of it." Or "I lost the people who were not real friends in the first place. They're gone now. The accident showed me who they truly were."

My revised thoughts accepted reality, rather than railing against reality. (When you pit yourself against reality, guess which one of you is going to lose?) When I made such mental adjustments, my thoughts switched from feeling like a victim of circumstance to feeling that maybe, just maybe, I could steer my future destiny.

Was it easy? No. It was probably the most difficult thing I have ever undertaken, as I had to fight the natural urge to just do nothing and let life sweep over me. It wasn't the easy option, but it was infinitely easier than the life I was experiencing at the time.

3)   Realise you're not giving in

I didn't need to give up or give in. I did need to move on and start afresh. I was determined to get away from the *why* of what happened, and into the *how* I was going to improve my life with the resources I had. I started picking up the pieces of my shattered life and put together a new picture. This picture included new friends, new interests, and new purpose.

I want you to know I did this, and so can you. It will be a struggle at first, as it was for me, but it gets easier with time. Have a look at your perception of the word "acceptance." Is it keeping you stuck because you equate it with giving up?

A sure sign you're not accepting things as they are will be that you're stuck in a cycle of ruminating about the past and projecting remorseful "if only" thoughts into the future. Your inner critic will be with you every inch of the way, tormenting you with thoughts of how things *used* to be.

4)   Make a commitment to change

Maybe it's time to accept that you must move on—not give up, but move on to a better, more fulfilling life. Does this change in your way of thinking work for all circumstances? No, it doesn't. There will always be exceptions to the rules. We are not a one-size-fits-all species. We are unique individuals with our own unique sets of problems. I would never presume to know your life better than you do.

But I would suggest you at least try on my recommendations for size. If it fits for you, then you have taken the first step to potentially changing your future. At the moment, you are probably stuck between the proverbial rock and hard place, trying to decide what to do. Consider taking the plunge and go with this radical new way of thinking I am describing. It certainly changed my life for the better. Maybe it will change yours, too.

5)   Realise acceptance is not forgiveness

Read those words and then read them again. Tattoo them on your forehead in reverse so you can read them when you look in the mirror.

Forgiveness is the stumbling block some people have a problem with when they think about acceptance. The fact of the matter is, it is quite possible to accept the way things are and not to forgive. Those two thoughts *can* occupy the same space; one doesn't depend on the other.

Our problems in the here and now are generally caused by our refusal to accept that things have changed and that our life is different. Acceptance is about getting real with the way things *actually* are, not how we would *like* them to be. We are trying and failing to influence something in our past or future which we have absolutely no control over. It has happened or is going to happen regardless of how much we would like the opposite to be true.

I would have liked my past not to have happened. Does this mean anything is going to change if I get angry or depressed? Definitely not.

6) Get out of your own way

If you are thinking to yourself, "So he expects me to just put up with my misfortune!" or "That worked for him, but there's not a chance it could possibly work for me," that means you have a bigger problem than I can help you with. It means you aren't willing to try. You're determined to keep things just the way they are. I don't know your reasons for wanting to keep the status quo in place, but there is always a reason.

With some people it is a way of gaining sympathy or attention. They have been doing the victim dance for so long that misery defines them. It gives meaning to their lives. It's part of their identity now.

Is it easy to accept your past? Is it easy to accept something happened you cannot change? Is it easy to let go of anger, bitterness, and vengeance? If you answered no, then ask yourself this: Is it easier to live with all the baggage you're carrying around? If the answer to that is also no, then what have you got to lose by letting it go?

It took me ten years, after my accident, before I understood the concept of acceptance completely. My wish for you is that it won't take the same long time. I trust that as you progress through this chapter, something will switch on in your mind, and you will see acceptance as a way of moving on with your life—no forgiveness required—and you won't see it as just another stick to beat yourself with. Time will tell.

Here is a little saying I created and live my own life by: If you can't accept *it,* then you are destined to be victimised by *it.*

7)   Don't drink the poison

If someone or something caused the problems you're now experiencing, either by design or accident, then getting bitter is like drinking poison and hoping the other person will keel over. They won't. They have forgotten you exist. They have moved on with their lives, and you are still the victim. Is it fair? No, it's not fair, but then again whoever said life was fair? Bad things happen to good people. Fact.

Okay then. I will assume I still have your attention and you are open to the possibility of changing and learning acceptance. What next?

8)   Talk to your subconscious mind

First, be open to the concept that you *can* change your reaction to your problems and get away from thoughts of "I have always been this way, therefore I cannot change." That way of thinking is a surefire way to stay stuck, possibly for the rest of your life. It can and does happen.

Your inner critic is looking for answers to such questions as "Why me?", "What have I done to deserve this?", and "Why is life so bad?" What I suggest is that you give your inner critic an answer to those questions in the form of a true statement, as follows: "I don't know why. It is what it is, for now."

The *for now* part of the statement is of vital importance as it tells the subconscious mind things *will* change eventually. Can you see how this works?

It's like an affirmation, and it works because it's true. You *don't* know the answers to those questions. Because the statement is true, the subconscious mind won't reject it, and when you say the situation is what it is *for now*, you are telling the subconscious mind that your being stuck is only temporary. Your subconscious takes things very literally. It doesn't know if *temporary* means six days or six years, but it understands you're saying that your being stuck is not permanent.

Ninety-nine percent of affirmations do not work because they are worded in a way that is not true. For example, if you say to yourself, "I am rich with a million dollars in my bank account," then unless you really have a million dollars in your bank account, all the subconscious mind will do is check to see if the statement is true, find that it's not, and reject the affirmation.

When you are answering, "It is what it is, for now," well, that is true. Another true statement you can answer your inner critic with is:

> **"Whatever happens, I will cope."**

This statement is also true because if you weren't coping (however badly), then you wouldn't be here. As you can see, there is no forgiveness required, just acceptance of what is, for now. Don't let reluctance to forgive block you from moving on with your life.

Will this little tool I've taught you help in all circumstances? I don't know because I'm not living your life. You won't know until you try it for yourself. But after all, the alternative—doing nothing—will keep you exactly where you are now.

And that's not what you want for yourself. It isn't a weakness to accept that your life has changed. What is a weakness is never to try to get your life back together.

9)   Realise it's never too late

Writing this chapter was surprisingly difficult for me. I never realised until I wrote it how much pain I had caused by not accepting that my life had changed beyond all recognition. Not only did it affect me, but everybody I knew as well. I had made everyone into a powerless victim, unable to help or to reach me. I wrote this chapter because I want to reach you in a way I was unable to be reached for a very long time.

You are not a powerless victim or a bystander in your own life. It's never too late to turn things around.

> **If you can't see the light at the end of the tunnel, it's because you are looking the other way. Shift your focus from what's *not* working.**

There has never been a better time to walk toward the light and leave the darkness behind. Use this book and my experiences as the catalyst for the change you have been waiting for. I am with you every inch of the way.

CHAPTER 8

Expectation

Okay, I think we both need a coffee break after the last chapter. You'll be relieved to know this one will be a lot lighter. So light in fact, I am not going to give you any advice. A few choices maybe, but not much advice. So put your feet up, relax, and enjoy the next few minutes, while I go and make a cup of tea. Please tell me you brought the tea bags. Did you not learn your lesson from the last time?

What do you expect to happen tomorrow morning? Do you expect to wake up breathing (always a good sign)? Do you expect the day to get brighter as the hours pass? Excellent, there is no reason you should not expect these things to happen. Ah, but wait. Will you also expect people to treat you the way you would like to be treated? To expect anything from another human being other than for them to be themselves always leads to disappointment. Certainly we would *like* other people to treat us as we would treat them, but expecting it to happen is another story.

Here's the strange thing about expectation: When things don't go as we expect, we turn it on ourselves. We make hurtful statements to ourselves, like "What's wrong with me? Why don't they like me?" or "I'm not good enough." The inner critic is having a great time at our expense. Somehow we manage to twist someone's actions or inaction into being our fault.

I want to share a different way of thinking with you. It will help change an automatic style of reacting to situations over which you have no control. It will also help you to see things the way they actually are, and not how you would prefer them to be.

We need to look at the word "expectation" a little more deeply before we can get around to changing your reaction to it. Hang in there. This will be worth it.

Expectation ... Your partner expects you to act a certain way, your work colleagues expect you to act a certain way, and your family expects you to act a certain way. The same also holds true for you. You expect people to act a certain way with you, and most likely you get upset when they don't.

Let's have a look at an example of a natural but unrealistic expectation of others and see if you recognise yourself. Let's say you have a friend you phone and talk to on a regular basis, and, of course, they do the same with you. For no apparent reason, they stop calling for three days. You start to get worried, then worry turns into annoyance and maybe even anger, but why?

The reason is actually quite straightforward: your expectation is they should call because it's what *you* would do. I hate to be the bearer of bad news (actually I don't, it doesn't bother me at all), but guess what? They aren't you, and you are not them. There is no rulebook apart from the one which exists inside our minds that says people should do what *we* think they should.

Let go of expecting things to happen in a certain way and instead adopt a policy of zero expectation of other people. You will certainly be a lot happier and won't be subject to your own self-inflicted disappointments. If you have high expectations of everybody and everything, you are going to go through life in a state of disillusionment, as humans have a bad habit of not living up to our self-imposed standards.

Here are just a few of the things most of us expect on a daily basis:

- We expect other people to treat us the way we think they should.

- We expect other drivers to be courteous.

- We expect to receive *that* phone call.

Can you see the pattern in the above list? Our expectations are based on another person's behaviour matching our rules. Unless they know and agree with our rules, they will not change their behaviour.

I'm going to suggest something radical. How about if you change your rules instead? Rather than expecting something to happen in a certain way, why not have zero expectations and see what happens?

A strange thing occurs when you lower your expectations. You notice and start to enjoy a new type of freedom. Why is it new? Because, for the first time in your life, you are free from trying to control something you have no control over: what other people do. The fact is, we have zero control over that anyway, so why not stop trying?

If we are upset or depressed at another person's behaviour, then this is our mind's attempt at controlling the situation based on our internal rulebook of standards. This is not to say you have to put up with rudeness or selfishness inflicted on you by someone; just don't expect them to change their behaviour if they don't see the problem. There is no need to get obnoxious or nasty. You will soon come to realise and see for yourself that other people are only one thing ... *not you.*

Examine any negative event surrounding your interaction with others, and you will come to understand that nine times out of ten it's about your natural but unrealistic expectations—expectations based on your own internal rule book of how things should be. Bring your expectations down to a realistic level and throw out your rulebook for a while. You will probably be amazed at how calm and content you will feel.

If you can't bring your expectations down, then you need to ask yourself why. Some people actually enjoy playing the role of victim and telling the world how selfish and rude other people are.

I would like to close this chapter with something for you to think about:

➤ **You can't be all things to all people. You can only be you.**

There will always be people who don't like you, don't approve of you, and have unrealistic expectations of you based on their own internal rulebook. Does this mean you're not good enough? I think you already know the answer.

CHAPTER 9

The Awareness Solution Technique

Master this technique, and you will have something you can use for the rest of your life. This is your next step on the road to inner awareness. The technique will give you insights into your own behaviour and the behaviour of others. It will clearly demonstrate when action is required to resolve an issue and when it is time to accept that sometimes we can't control an outcome, however much we would like the opposite to be true.

To obtain maximum benefit from the awareness solution, you will need to be honest with yourself. It's so easy to fool ourselves into thinking, "No that's not the real problem", or "It doesn't apply to me". People do this to avoid facing reality. Does this sound like you? If so, my advice is to be brave and face that reality.

I devised the solution as a way of bringing something which is subconscious into conscious awareness, where it can be dealt with. The solution can be used on its own or in combination with the other chapters in this book.

Our usual way of dealing with emotions and feelings is to *put up and shut up*—it is what we were taught. A display of emotion was considered a weakness to be hidden at all costs.

The only problem with putting up and shutting up is we are denying the problem exists. The inner critic will not accept such a solution; it will always find a way for the problem to bubble to the surface again. One percent of the time our problems *are* insurmountable, and there *isn't* an answer. The awareness solution is designed for the other ninety-nine percent.

Begin by identifying the uncomfortable emotion you are experiencing. Is it fear? Anger? Anxiety? Sadness? Something else?

Next, determine if the emotion is related to the past, present, or future. You do this by asking yourself three questions about the past, the same three questions about the present, and the same three questions about the future.

Here are the questions:

- What am I trying to change or influence?
- Whose behaviour am I trying to change or influence?
- Can I do something about it, or do I need to accept it?

Past, present, and future—all problems we have are located within these three areas. Seems obvious, doesn't it? It is obvious until I ask you, "Why are you upset?" You will more than likely answer, "I don't know, I just feel annoyed and angry." The fact is *something* is bubbling away, eating at you—probably your inner critic.

To find out *what* it is, we need to get specific. This is where the awareness solution technique comes into its own. It enables us to be very specific, but first we have to find out where the problem resides.

So after identifying the emotion, you begin surveying the past. Ask yourself the following:

- What am I trying to change or influence in my past?
- Whose behaviour am I trying to change or influence in my past?
- Can I do something about it, or do I need to accept it?

Using the same questions, you then do a review of the present:

- What am I trying to change or influence in my present?
- Whose behaviour am I trying to change or influence in my present?
- Can I do something about it, or do I need to accept it?

Finally, you look to the future:

- What am I trying to change or influence in my future?
- Whose behaviour am I trying to change or influence in my future?
- Can I do something about it, or do I need to accept it?

Querying yourself in this manner helps you to consciously pinpoint what it is that is troubling you. It also helps you assume a healthy attitude about the matter and step out of the stressing mindset.

For the sake of example, let's say you have determined that the emotion bothering you is worry and that it is located in the future. You are concerned about an upcoming event—your daughter's wedding—it's making you nervous.

You ask yourself:

- What am I trying to change or influence in my future?

   I am trying and failing to control something I have no control over. My daughter's wedding is going to happen in three weeks, whether I'm ready or not.

- Whose behaviour am I trying to change or influence in my future?

   I am trying to influence my daughter's behaviour. I am projecting into a future which has not happened yet, causing me anxiety and imagining all the terrible things that could go wrong with the wedding.

- Can I do something about it, or do I need to accept it?

I can give my daughter encouragement and advice, but I cannot control her choices and actions about her own wedding. I can take action on my own to a degree, but then I must accept what she decides. I don't have to like it, just to accept it. Once I do that, I can stop fighting with myself and my daughter and can move on.

We cannot control the behaviour of another human, we can only control our reaction to it. Sometimes we just have to accept that another person's behaviour is not what we'd like it to be. If we try to get them to change, it normally results in an escalation of the problem.

Can you see how it works? The power lies in the simplicity of the questions. They help you to hone in on what is really bothering you, then deal with the problem by responding in a healthy, realistic manner.

Please note I never said any potential solutions were going to be easy. The awareness solution allows you to recognise there *are* alternatives to putting up and shutting up.

I want to finish by giving you a real-life example of the awareness solution at work. It happened in a one-on-one session with a client in my private therapy practice. This man was taking heart medication and was literally dying from stress. His job was literally killing him, but he was afraid of letting people down and looking bad.

Stress is another form of anxiety, so his problems were all based in the future. So I asked the questions:

- What event are you trying to influence or change in the future?

- Whose behaviour are you trying to influence?

- Can you do something about it, or do you need to accept it?

The first question was met with this answer: "I am trying to prevent myself from dying."

The second question was answered: "I am trying to influence what people think of me."

The third question was answered: "I have to change or leave my job before it kills me, and also drop the notion that I can control what people think."

There is a lot more to this story, but suffice it to say the client left his job and is now living happily, not really caring what anybody thinks. We can inflict a lot of damage on ourselves when we are obsessed by other people's opinions. The simple fact is, people will think what they want. You have no way of controlling it, so you might as well accept it. If you have a method to control other people's thoughts, I wish you well. You will make millions.

So that is the complete technique. It is simple to implement and can give insights you never thought were there, but only if you are honest with your answers.

So to recap:

- Identify the emotion: Is it fear, anger, frustration? Give it a name.

- Identify its location: Is it in the past, present, or future?

- Ask yourself the questions, and be truthful with the answers.

Before you go, I have a little tip you might find helpful. Why not buy yourself three fridge magnets: the letter P for past, another letter P for present, and the letter F for future? Place the letters somewhere you can see them every day. They will serve as a reminder to use the technique, instead of putting up and shutting up.

I am sure you could probably think of other reminders that would have the same effect. After a while you won't need the reminders, but for now they can serve as a gentle nudge in the right direction.

CHAPTER 10

Acknowledge Small Steps of Courage

Have you ever noticed how quick we are to beat ourselves up for the slightest little thing which doesn't live up to our expectations of how we think things should be? It seems to be like a national pastime; we admonish ourselves quickly and with venom for the slightest infraction of our own self-imposed rules and values. We are our own harshest critic; we say things to ourselves, which if someone else said to us, would put them in hospital for a month. I want to change this. First I would like to ask you a question. How many times have you rewarded yourself for a job well done? I can answer the question for you. If you are being honest, probably very close to zero.

As you already know, the rest of the book is devoted to techniques and strategies to help you make peace with your inner critic. This short but important chapter concentrates on making those same techniques and strategies stronger and more effective.

So how is it possible to obtain *maximum* benefit from all you are learning in this book? You obtain maximum benefit by acknowledging the small courageous steps you are taking toward your ultimate goal. It doesn't matter if your goal is gaining more confidence or being more accepting, or maybe even committing to resolving your depression. All that matters is you are moving courageously in the right direction, and that fact should be acknowledged.

Why is it so important to acknowledge ourselves? Because a very curious thing happens when you reward yourself for achievement. Your brain releases the feel-good chemical dopamine into your bloodstream. Dopamine is a naturally occurring chemical in your brain. Its scientific name is 4-(2-amininoethyl) benzyne-1,2-diol, and there is no reason for telling you that other than to make me look intelligent (I googled it). It is released anytime you reward yourself. You experience it off and on for most of the day. Let's do a little thought exercise so you can recognise how it feels.

Close your eyes. No not yet, wait for it. Close your eyes and imagine or remember the last time you did something that made you happy or that you felt proud of. An example could be the birth of your children or maybe even the feelings of closeness you associate with someone you love. Really get into the spirit of things and remember how that feels. Hold that experience for about thirty seconds and then open your eyes again. That feel good feeling is dopamine being released. Felt good, didn't it?

When we reward ourselves our brain releases that feel-good chemical to encourage us to repeat the behaviour, thus reinforcing it and turning it into a potentially positive habit. Now you know why having sex and eating feels so good, but maybe not both at the same time. So the next time someone asks, "Why are you smiling" you can tell them it's the naturally occurring chemical 4-(2-aminoethyl) benzyne-1,2-diol in your bloodstream and you can't help yourself. That should impress them.

The reward doesn't have to take the form of a street party, just a quiet recognition for a job well-done. I want you to make an association in your brain:

> **Facing the fear and doing it anyway equals reward and feeling good.**

Keep repeating the technique I am going to share with you of rewarding yourself for achievement (no matter how small) until rewarding yourself becomes a habit. You will have learned a new skill which is transferrable to any intimidating situation you would like to master.

The technique is so simple to use. The hardest thing will be remembering to actually use it. (Maybe you can come up with a way to remind yourself.)

Let's imagine that getting confident with strangers is the goal you want to achieve. If you don't have such confidence, the act of talking to someone you don't know can be a daunting experience. Let's say, you face the fear and do it anyway: you muster your courage and talk to a stranger.

What you do next is of vital importance: you reward yourself for a job well-done. You don't need to get out the party streamers. All you need to do is say quietly into yourself:

> **"Well done. I did that".**

It only takes a few seconds to do, and your brain will appreciate the dopamine bath. This phrase is only a suggestion of what you might say to yourself. Please feel free to come up with something more personal to you, to use as an achievement statement of your own.

I completely understand if at this point you are thinking, "Giving myself a compliment won't solve my problem." You would be one hundred percent correct. This technique is not for solving problems. It is, however, a powerful way of adding strength to every small step of courage you are taking toward solving a problem. Don't be fooled by its simplicity. Try it and see.

CHAPTER 11

Ten Ways to Change Your Behaviour

Changing your own behaviour is rarely as simple as just going for it, regardless of what you might have read to the contrary. Normally what happens when we just go for it is we get disheartened and disillusioned when we run into an unexpected mind trap. Changing your own behaviour is actually a quite straightforward process *if* you are prepared for what lies ahead. I have noticed over the years of both working with clients and in my own personal life there are ten potential obstacles to be aware of. With those in mind, I've devised ten steps for successfully making the change in your life you desire.

1)   Ask yourself what you actually want

Seems like an obvious thing to do, doesn't it? In fact, the vast majority of people can tell you what they don't want, but they have never given much thought to what they actually do want. For instance, saying, "I don't want to be overweight" is quite different than saying "I want to weigh 140 pounds". The first statement leaves your mind and motivation stranded, as it is so general. The second statement is specific and detailed. Your subconscious mind loves specifics and details, as it can go to work on these to find a solution. It hates generalisations and unspecific goals; if it is given a generalisation, it will more than likely give you a roadblock in return. Have a look at these next two statements, and consider which is the most likely to motivate the subconscious mind into action:

- I don't want to be depressed.

- I want to be happy.

Obviously statement two is going to have the most chance of success, as it is something you want. Use this information to answer your own question, *"What do I want?"* Just get started. You don't need to know the precise answer straightaway. It will come to you as you progress toward your goal. If you're having problems even starting, you might find it helpful to re-read Chapter 4: "Are You Premeditating Failure?".

2)   Enlist the help of others

Once you've determined what you want, consider who you might ask to help you. If you want to be more self-confident, perhaps there's a friend you can ask for advice. If the issue concerns your health, your doctor might be an excellent resource. Be extremely cautious using online forums for advice on mental health. You will rarely find an answer; you will, however, find a lot of miserable people. Not so good if you are suffering from depression. It's time to take some action. Enlisting the help of real people is a great way to start moving forward. They are also a resource for getting feedback on your progress. I have found people love to help, if only you ask.

3) Don't search for meaning that isn't there

Asking yourself "Why me?" or "What have I done to deserve this?" is a futile waste of your precious time as you are sending your mind on a journey it can't complete. Asking yourself these questions will cause paralysis by analysis and keep you stuck.

> ➤ **It doesn't matter how you got to this point, what matters is what you do next.**

If I were able to answer the question "why" for you, it wouldn't make the slightest bit of difference as the issue would still remain. Education does not cause resolution, action does. Sometimes things just happen for no apparent reason. Sometimes bad things happen to good people. It isn't fair, but that doesn't make it any less true.

Think about this for a moment: if you *were* able to answer the question "Why me?", what would you do after that? How about acting *as if* you do know the answer, and see what happens?

4) Make it smaller

When we want to change a behaviour, it can seem overwhelming. We're inclined to look at the overall picture and feel swamped. We think about how long it is going to take and then give up before we even start. I want you to try something different. Divide the

80

goal up into the smallest pieces possible, then decide on the smallest first step you can take, and begin.

As the old joke goes, "How do you eat an elephant? One bite at a time." When you look at the goal as a whole, it seems huge and insurmountable, but if you view it from the perspective of many small actions, it can seem quite doable.

And that's how you master the overwhelm factor of having a big goal. By way of illustration, consider this example: if your goal is to exercise more and you do just ten minutes of exercise a day, by the time a year has passed you will have done approximately sixty hours of exercise. If you were to remove two pieces of chocolate from your diet per day (200 calories), over a year that would add up to 72,000 calories.

Get the idea? Divide it down into tiny steps and get started. The important part is not how you begin, but actually beginning. The details you can work on later.

5)   Change for yourself

When we want to change a problematic behaviour, the chances of success are remote, unless we are doing it for ourselves. If we try to change our behaviour for someone else's benefit, we can run into problems. Other people can certainly benefit from our behaviour change, but they can't keep us motivated for the long haul.

I want you to try something radically different, I want you to spend the next five minutes thinking about the reasons *why* you want to change your behaviour, and then make sure the reasons are about *you* and no one else. Be totally selfish; you have to be if you are serious about change. Pick out the main reason for changing, and keep it foremost in your mind. This is what will keep you motivated if times get tough; it has to be about *you*.

6)   Anticipate setbacks

Wouldn't it be great if we could just think about changing a behaviour and everything went perfectly, and the change took place as if by magic? Yes, it would, but we live in the real world. Life sometimes gets in the way of our best intentions, no matter how focused we are. I want you to put some thought into what you will do if you suffer a setback. Most people don't even consider having a setback, and what happens? Their mind takes the path of least resistance and returns to the old behaviour, all because they hadn't prepared for the inevitable.

For instance, it is quite a common occurrence for smokers to say, "I took one cigarette, so I thought I might as well stop trying." My answer would be, "What about the ten thousand you didn't smoke for the last six months, do they not count?" Think ahead and be aware that setbacks are part of being human. Then prepare for them.

This way it won't come as a shock if it happens. Preparation is the key to successful behaviour change.

Forewarned is forearmed so they say. Anticipating problems and finding solutions is hardwired into your very being; why not use your brain in the way it was created to be used? The fact is, setbacks are going to arise no matter how much you would like the opposite to be true.

If you were driving from A to B and got lost, would you just give up and go home? No, of course you wouldn't. You would correct your course and get back on track again. The same rules apply here; there is no need to beat yourself up over something that happened unexpectedly. Just see it for what it is: a detour.

Your attitude to setbacks will determine how long it takes to get things moving forward again. You can choose to see yourself as the helpless victim, or you can ask, "How do I get things moving again?"

> **If you have a dream and don't anticipate setbacks, then all you have is a dream.**

7) Don't fool yourself

In previous chapters I have used the term "cognitive dissonance" a few times. Put simply, cognitive dissonance is another word for an excuse, and this excuse allows you to maintain a behaviour without feeling bad or guilty about it.

I will give you a few examples, to make things clearer:

- I need to smoke as it helps me relax.
- I have always been heavy because I am big-boned.
- I can't do xyz because I don't have the time.
- It is rude to say no.

When we use cognitive dissonance to maintain a behaviour, we are also playing the role of helpless victim. We are saying what is happening to us is outside our control and we are powerless. Sometimes it might actually be true, but the majority of the time it isn't. We are keeping a behaviour in place instead of changing it because it is easier to do so.

If you are using cognitive dissonance and trying to change a behaviour at the same time, your chances of success are zero. I recognise that sounds a bit harsh, but it's true. You also know it's true, and it probably made you feel uncomfortable. Which is a good thing, because now you recognise it's what *you* have been doing.

So how do we remove cognitive dissonance? We take responsibility and recognise it for what it is—an excuse—and then commit to stop using it. Let me put it another way. If you don't stop using your favourite excuse, you are going to be stuck with the behaviour—maybe for the rest of your life.

To make any progress, which is what we all want, it's time to choose one or the other: the excuse or the behaviour you want. There are no third options or grey areas. Cognitive dissonance is a real dream stopper; it keeps us stuck in a nice little comfort zone we have created for ourselves. When we are saying to ourselves, "I would like to, but …", then it's time to stop using excuses and start taking some action.

8) Recognise your fears

Do you remember when you first got behind the wheel of a car to learn to drive? All those switches and pedals and having to remember a thousand things at once. It was probably the most terrifying experience you ever had. It was frightening because you were out of your comfort zone and in unknown territory. A few years later, and you can drive a car nearly on autopilot. You didn't find bravery from somewhere, you just adapted to a new skill until it became automatic. Making changes in your life is done in exactly the same way; we face our fears and then we adapt.

What is it about change that scares us so much? The very thought sends shivers down our spines. Is it the hard work? Do we feel we are not up to the task? We are creatures of our own evolution, and evolution helps to control what we will and won't do. Imagine living tens of thousands of years ago. The world would have been a very different place. We lived in tribes of thirty to thirty-five, and we all depended on each other. If we were rejected from our tribe, it meant certain death. Fast forward to modern-day existence, and we are still carrying the fear of rejection with us.

Fortunately today we don't usually have to worry about certain death if we are rejected, but the fear is there nonetheless. We fear success, we fear failure, we stay in our comfort zone, we stay safe and nothing changes. If you want to change anything in your behaviour, you have to confront these fears. Despite what you have read elsewhere, real change is not something that happens magically just by thinking about it. Comfort zones have to be expanded slowly; we have to recognise our fears before we can push through them.

Think about what your greatest fear of change is. It will probably lose its power when you think about it for a few minutes. Question your fears. Are they real or imaginary? Can you get what you want and still feel scared while you pursue it? Of course you can.

9) Identify your saboteurs

I have found almost anyone can sabotage our efforts, either deliberately or by accident, especially in the early days of our transition. For instance, someone might invite you to a restaurant even though you are trying to lose weight; it isn't done deliberately to sabotage you, but the end result can still be the same. It's just something you need to be aware of and plan for.

Here is something counterintuitive: some people you come into contact with regularly won't necessarily applaud your new change of behaviour, as they will find it difficult to adapt to the change in you. The people you really need to be aware of are the ones who would like you to keep things the same as they have always been.

What is going unsaid here is, "If I can't do it, I don't want you doing it," so it shouldn't come as any surprise when someone tries to derail you. Most of the time there is no malice intended; it's simply because you are holding a mirror up to their own perceived weaknesses and making them feel uncomfortable. Smokers and overeaters are particularly prone to this type of behaviour. Watch out for the "Just one won't do you any harm", "You're okay the way you are", or "Why bother?" statements. Only you can decide who has your best interests at heart, and act accordingly.

10) Get started now

The subconscious mind is where all your behaviours live. It first learned—by repetition—the problematic behaviour you now want to drop, and it will learn the new behaviour in exactly the same way. Repetition and practice are the *only* ways to learn a new behaviour. There is no book you can read or course you can take to shortcut this process. It's something you have to go through, which at times can be tough. You have to be aware of and monitor your new behaviours until they become automatic. This will take time, but the rewards will be well-worth the effort. If you have a setback, see it for what it is and not as a reason to give up altogether.

The road from wherever you are now to wherever you want to go will never be a straight line. If you understand this to be a fact, then you won't be disappointed when you hit a diversion. You will just find a way around it.

Actually, there is a number eleven (sneaky, I know)

I want you to get the maximum-possible benefit from the preceding ten tips. So, please give what follows some serious consideration before turning the page. I strongly recommend you do something within the next thirty minutes to commit yourself to changing your behaviour. If you don't, I can predict with a fair degree of accuracy you won't make the change at all.

This is not something I made up; it's just how your brain works. It can be as simple as sending yourself a text stating when you are going to start, even putting a circle around a date on a calendar counts; do something, anything, but do it now.

By my reckoning there are twenty-nine minutes left, so I will finish the way I started by asking you the question, "What now?" Don't listen to your inner critic, which doesn't want you to change.

Don't wait until the time feels right, because it will never feel right. Just get started. Make the commitment. You won't regret it.

CHAPTER 12

Going for a Goal

Now let's talk about some crucial steps required for achieving any goal you have in mind. It doesn't matter if the goal is more confidence, more money, weight loss, or to become comfortable speaking in public—the steps are exactly the same. (I am hoping by this stage in the book you already know what you want.)

I think to make reading easier, we shall concentrate on getting more money as our hypothetical goal. But the same techniques can be applied to any goal you set. So let's proceed, with money as the example, and look at what the six steps are to creating a workable goal:

1) Focus on your goal

It's important to word your goal using specific language. "More money" may seem like a good goal, but the focus is flawed. How much is more? Do you want to earn an extra dollar a week? Probably not. You need to decide (and to say or write down) exactly what it is that you're after.

How about "Ten billion dollars". Is that a good goal? Well, the subconscious mind might reject that goal because it does not seem "true". Ten billion dollars is probably such a stretch from the amount of money you have right now, that it is unbelievable.

So let's revise the goal to make it believable. How about "Fifteen thousand dollars more this year than last year"? Is that a good, focused goal? Yes, because it says exactly what you want, and it's not so massive as to sound unrealistic to your subconscious mind. (If you want ten billion dollars, you can, of course, keep making new goals once your smaller goal is reached. The point is not to aim for the stars before you've even hit the first fifty-yard bull's-eye.)

2)   Develop a plan

Once you've decided what your goal is, the next step is to make a realistic plan for achieving it. Are you going to change your job? Get a second job? Create an online business? What will be the business you create, or the job you are going to change to or add? This is the level of detail you need to go into to have any chance of success.

At this point I diverge from the normal self-help advice given. Let's say your goal was to acquire $100,000. Instead of thinking, "How do I acquire $100,000", I want you to think, "How do I acquire $1,000?" If you can't work out a plan to acquire

$1,000, then $100,000 will be setting you up for failure before you even start.

If we can acquire $1,000, then we have achieved the first step and tasted success. All we need to do now is build on this success. It's a lot easier on your brain to process small steps than to be overwhelmed with what seems like an impossible task. Does this mean you can't go after the $100,000? No, it just means you hold the idea of the big-money goal softly. But move forward with manageable and realistic steps. You *have* to walk before you can run.

Holding an idea softly means not obsessing about the end result. You know it's something you want, but it's in the back of your mind, not the front. The *process* of how to achieve what you want should be your only concern. Think of it as a journey, not a destination.

"Get all the money you want in thirty days" makes a great book title, but in the real world getting or changing anything requires persistence and a bit of willpower.

3)   Be "the sort of person"

We humans have a tendency to think we're not up to the task if a goal pushes us out of our comfort zone. It's very normal and common to feel overwhelmed before we even start, especially if the task is perceived as difficult. We need to find a way around triggering fear, which causes inaction.

Let me give you a few examples:

- I'm not the sort of person who could acquire $100,000

   But I am the sort of person who could acquire $1000 and build on it.

- I'm not the sort of person who could speak in public.

   But I am the sort of person who could practice with friends and build on it.

- I'm not the sort of person who could lose a hundred pounds.

   But I am the sort of person who could lose twenty-five pounds, and maybe more sets of twenty-five after that.

- I'm not the sort of person who is confident around strangers.

   But I am the sort of person who could practice with one stranger at a time.

Can you see how this works? You take the initial thought of what you want (the big picture) and make it smaller and more manageable until you reach whatever your goal happens to be. This may fly in the face of other things you have read, but let me ask you a question. If it is so easy to obtain something by just setting a goal and going after it, then why aren't we all rich, confident, happy individuals? The reason is fear: fear of failure, fear of being judged, fear of rejection.

All of those fears are potential obstacles in your path if you don't know how to deal with them.

If you are the sort of person who can still push forward despite these fears, then you have my admiration. If you are not, then congratulations—you are not alone; most of us feel the same way. I'm striving to give you a template which will enable you to remove fear from swallowing your goal. Take these suggestions and adapt them to your way of thinking; it will then be your template and not mine. You will stand a greater chance of success by making the process your own.

4)   Take the first small step

What is the first small step you can take in obtaining your goal? Do you need to make a phone call, go on the Internet, ask friends for advice, buy a book? What do you need to do first to get things moving forward? Think small. Get into the fine details. Write it down so you won't forget it.

When you write something down, you give your mind a message to take seriously whatever you commit to on paper. Your subconscious mind can process four million pieces of information a second. Committing something to paper has the effect of engaging the handbrake. It slows things down long enough for your mind to get the message, "This is serious".

You don't need to know all the answers in advance, and trying to think ten steps ahead will throw your mind into overload. This is the greatest obstacle to achieving what you want. Think "walk", not "run". Taking one step at a time is a very effective way of achieving your goal. If you run, you will more than likely fall over your own feet.

Let me give you a personal example from my experience of building a house. When I decided to build a house (something I said I would never do), I also went into overload. My mind went wild with questions:

- How do I find a builder?

- How much money will it take?

- How do I start?

- How do I end?

- Who will design it?

- Etc., etc., etc.

All these questions had one thing in common: They were all currently outside my control and influence. I was projecting into a future which did not exist. I took control of the only thing I had control over: me. I took a leap of faith, believing all the answers I didn't have would eventually show up, and they did.

I'm hoping you will do the same. Take the leap of faith, and eventually your questions will be answered, too. For now just go with the flow. Take one question at a time, and work with it. Don't project off into a thousand different directions; otherwise, you will be overwhelmed into inaction. Start from the position "I can do this" to give yourself the best chance of being successful.

5)   Keep it to yourself, for now

Here I go diverging again. Nearly every book I have read says to tell everybody about your plans. Supposedly this will keep you on track to achieving your goal. With some people this might actually be true. I am going to give you an alternative, and explain why letting the world know your plans might not be the best course of action.

I completely agree you *should* tell your nearest and dearest what you are proposing. Even then, only tell those you absolutely know will support you. Remember this is about what *you* want; it is not a spectator sport where everyone gets to have an opinion on what you should do.

When you tell people what you propose to do, you will receive one of two reactions. They will either support you completely, or they will try to discourage you or to talk you out of it. It's the second group you should be interested in, as they might have a vested interest in wanting to see you fail. They could be jealous, or you might be making them feel insecure. It doesn't really matter what the reason is, these people are toxic to your goal.

Here's why you should avoid telling such people your plans:

95

- You really don't need the extra layer of pressure.

- Do you want to have to justify your actions on a daily basis?

When making changes in our lives, we seek approval from others, especially in the early days of our plan. The downside of this is not everyone has our best interests at heart. It's unfortunate, but true nonetheless. Sometimes even good friends, who consciously wish only the best for us, will unconsciously try to sabotage our efforts. After all, if we succeed where they have failed, it makes them feel like more of a failure. So be wary: not all of your friends are friends of your goal.

Can you decipher fact from opinion? This is what you will have to be able to do the more people you tell about your plans. The more folks you tell, the more you will have to be able to do this. Trust your intuition. Anyone telling you what to do is giving you their opinion based on their own internal standards. Do you really want to live *your* life based on someone's opinion? Opinions are like birthdays, everybody's got one.

The good news is, when your plan is a bit further down the line, you can tell whomever you want to about it. By that time you will have seen proof your methods are working, and won't really care what anyone thinks.

I know in *theory* telling everybody what you are doing seems like a good idea, but in practice I have seen many clients derailed by seemingly well-intentioned friends and relatives. This was especially true for my weight-loss-therapy clients, who were already dealing with emotional issues. They couldn't cope with the fact that not everyone had the emotional investment in their future which they had. Not everyone will like what you are doing, which is their problem, not yours.

6)   Focus intently on the here and now

I have to diverge from the norm again, but it is for a very good reason. Most of what you have read about getting what you want in life probably said to focus intently on the future as if it has already happened ... imagining yourself as already having achieved your goal, visualising yourself exactly where you want to be.

I'll tell you why I think this is a bad idea. Your subconscious mind cannot tell the difference between something vividly imagined and reality. Horror films are a great example of this. You know logically what you are watching isn't real, but you still get frightened. Even if you think about the film a week later, you can still feel scared. Your imagination is driving the emotion you are feeling. It's as if you are there, and your body responds accordingly.

So when you vividly imagine yourself having achieved your goal, the subconscious mind will take the foot off the gas, so to speak. The reason it will do this is because your brain uses twenty percent of the calories you consume in a day. As far as it is concerned, the goal has been achieved, therefore precious resources can be diverted elsewhere.

I want to offer you an alternative: visualise going through the step you are currently engaged in. Don't visualise the outcome, just the process. I think you will find this a very viable alternative. Test it and see for yourself. As a matter of fact, test everything I tell you and see if it works for you. Then adapt it to your life and lifestyle as you see fit. Just remember to use the last chapter in combination with this chapter, as together they will be an immense help in getting from where you are now to where you want to be.

I won't wish you luck, as no part of this process relies on it. It relies on you persisting until you get to wherever it is you want to go.

Oh, okay then. Good luck.

CHAPTER 13

Changing Someone Else's Behaviour

Can trying to get someone to change a negative behaviour possibly do any harm? It can't, so long as the change is what they want, not what only you want. A few years ago a relative of mine (who we shall call Robert to protect his identity) was suffering from mild depression. He seemed to stumble from one problem to another, or so he told me.

Strange thing was, he never seemed to do anything to move forward with his life. He was resigned to believing that the current status quo was how things would continue. Anyhow, Robert was very lucky—I was a freshly minted therapist. I was going to come into his life and change his world. I had my Superman cape ready, and I was going to rescue him from himself … or so I naively thought.

I tried everything, and I mean everything, to get Robert's life back into some semblance of normality. All my efforts were met with a brick wall of resistance; he refused any and all help. I started to get frustrated and depressed myself. My inner critic made me start doubting my ability as an effective therapist. For some reason he just wanted to be left alone to continue as he saw fit. So what did I do? I couldn't just leave him to sort himself out ... or could I?

When the penny finally dropped with me, that's exactly what I did. I left him alone to live his life the way he wanted, because I had come to a stunning conclusion: I was trying to force him to do what I wanted, not what he wanted.

Not only that, I was harming myself in the process. Are you doing the same? Do you have someone in your life you are trying to rescue? By all means be there for them if they ask for your help, but stop playing the role of rescuer, as eventually that will harm you.

Trying to change someone else's behaviour is a noble idea, but it doesn't always work in the real world, and it can potentially leave you feeling angry, frustrated, and depressed. Trying to get another human being to change has got to be one of the hardest and most thankless things a person can do. A major downside is the potential feeling of inadequacy it can trigger. You can leave yourself feeling powerless and helpless if you try to change something you have no control over.

Worse still, you can trigger your own inner critic to make statements like, "If they loved me, they would change", or "They don't care about me, otherwise they would stop what they are doing". It is so easy to get caught up in this thinking. We can twist someone else's behaviour into meaning they don't love us, or into it somehow being our fault.

What is it about other people's actions that can upset us so much? We point out the obvious, we give them all the reasons why they should change. What happens? Nothing. Why does nothing happen? Are they stupid or arrogant or do they just not care?

The reason nothing happens is simple: they are not you. Never have been, never will be. Accepting this as a fact will make it easier for all concerned. Why does someone not change their behaviour in the way you would like? Because It's what you want, not what they want.

A person will only change if they think there is a problem. You can point out all the reasons why they should change, but if they don't accept them, you're talking to the wind. As an example: has any smoker—in the face of overwhelming evidence as to how dangerous it is—ever stopped smoking when they didn't want to? I very much doubt it; the reverse is true, and they will give you all the reasons why they should keep smoking. It helps with stress, it helps them relax, blah blah blah. I want you to repeat the next sentence as often as it takes for you to get the message:

> **I cannot change someone else's behaviour, I can only change my reaction to it.**

"But it isn't fair", I hear you say. And you might be right. But it is still a fact of life.

Governments have been trying for years to change people's behaviour. Just think of the drink/drive campaigns, the seatbelt campaigns, and the mobile-phone-while-driving campaigns. Can you imagine how many deaths would occur on the roads today if the power of choice was given to the individual? We normally only change our behaviour for one of two reasons:

- It is in our own best interest to do so.

- We are forced to and penalised hard if we don't.

I'm trying to keep you from wasting your time on something which is futile and will ultimately make you and the person concerned unhappy. There is every possibility you do know what is best for the person on occasion. If the person concerned doesn't get to make their own mistakes, they will just see your intervention as interference. Try to remember back to when you were younger. I am quite sure your parents told you not to do something, and then you went and did the complete opposite. (I know I did, but maybe I am the only one.)

They were trying to make you change your behaviour, and what happened? You performed the exact behaviour you were told not to. The same can potentially happen if you are doing this with an adult. If you try to get them to change and they can't see why they should, then an escalation of the same behaviour can result.

What about seeing this from a different angle? Can you separate the behaviour from the person in your own mind? It is very easy to get caught up in thinking, "If this person performs this behaviour, it makes them a bad person." No, it doesn't. The behaviour you don't like is only a very small part of who they are.

> **If possible, accept their behaviour as something they do, not who they are. You don't need to like or condone it.**

If you can separate the behaviour from the person, you will be a lot happier as you can see things for how they actually are and not how you would like them to be. If you can't, then you might want to review your relationship with that person. This is never going to be easy, but neither is being accused of interfering all the time.

We are not here to rescue people from themselves—life's too short for that kind of frustration. Sometimes we can't help people despite our best efforts. It's part of being human; we all have the ability to choose our own path.

Here's a sobering thought: Sometimes people don't want to be rescued. They have played the role of victim for so long it has become part of their identity. Giving up their behaviour would mean giving up something which gives meaning to their lives.

Behaviour is only the symptom. Every behaviour is driven by a belief. You are only seeing the external manifestation of the belief. Put simply, if someone is performing a behaviour, they are doing so for a reason and they are also deriving a benefit from it. This might seem like an alien concept to you because you are seeing things from your perspective.

Let me give a few examples to illustrate my point:

- Drinking to excess is a means of escaping reality. It also gives false confidence to someone who lacks confidence.

- Bullying is a way of dominating others in order to feel better about yourself.

- Sarcasm is a way of covering up chronic shyness.

- Arrogance is a way of disguising insecurity.

- Overeating can be used to suppress emotion.

Can you see that in order for the person to stop doing the behaviour, other needs have to be met? Unless you can meet those unfulfilled needs, what chance do you stand of getting them to drop the behaviour? If a person drinks to excess to give their confidence a boost so they can converse with members of the opposite sex, what do you think will happen if they stop drinking? I am not condoning any of the behaviours. I am trying to help you see how futile it is to try to get someone to drop a behaviour unless you have a plan in place to meet their unfulfilled needs.

Do you really want to plan someone else's life for them? I didn't think so. If you are aware that human beings are by their very nature contradictory, it will help you immensely. Then you won't have to beat yourself up when they refuse your best intentions to help them.

So what became of Robert? He went about his daily life as normal, still depressed. About a year later he actually came to me for help. Sometimes it's best just letting a situation take its natural course, no matter how painful it can be to watch.

CHAPTER 14

I Should, You Should

Try as I might, I can't think of anything positive to say about the word "should". If it is said to you in the form of "you should", then the person making the statement wants you to conform to *their* own internal standards and rules. If we are saying "I should" to ourselves, then it will ensure we can never be content and will always have feelings of never being good enough and somehow falling short all the time. "Should" is an empty word which has the ability to make us feel bad, even when there is no reason to.

When the words "you should" are said by another, there is always something which remains unsaid, but it is there nonetheless. Have a look at the list below for a few examples to see what I mean:

- You should lose some weight.

   I want you to lose some weight.

- You should stop smoking.

   I want you to stop smoking.

- You should get out more often.

I want you to get out more often.

Can you see how the word should has been dressed up to look like the other person is "only trying to help"? When in actual fact what they really want is for you to conform to their standards. It's subtle, but it is there. To counteract someone else's *"you should"* just ask them "Why should I?"

Expect a reaction; if you ask "Why should I?", the person making the statement won't have thought this through, and you will be challenging their standards. They will more than likely splutter something like "Because I said so", or something as equally ridiculous.

There are times when *"you should"* can be helpful, for example: "You should go a different route to avoid the traffic." I will assume you can tell the difference between information and subtle manipulation.

Another subtle implication of "you should" is we are somehow lacking and the other person knows us better than we know ourselves. Think about this before you are tempted to utter those words to someone else, as no one likes to be thought of as somehow lacking. If you are feeling particularly adventurous, when someone says "You should do xyz", just say, "Yes, I must do that" and then do precisely nothing. They will soon get tired of giving advice and getting nowhere.

A word of warning: if you are a teenager living at home reading this, then do as you are told, since the ramifications of not doing so can be far-reaching and painful. Don't be tempted to be a smart-ass; Mum and Dad know best ... you have been warned.

Now we come to the most corrosive statement of all which is "I should". If there are two words guaranteed to make us unhappy and discontent, then these two words are at the top of the list. They have the unique ability to keep us stuck in a rut and at the same time make us feel somehow lacking.

Let's have a look at some "I should" statements most commonly used:

- I *should* be happier.

- I *should* have more money.

- I *should* lose weight.

- I *should* stop smoking.

The "I should" statement on the face of it sounds like something you would think would be motivating and helpful, so why isn't it? The reason it isn't is because "I should" is an identity statement about yourself where a vital part of the statement is also missing.

Let me give you an example based on the previous list adding the unspoken words:

- I *should* be happier, *but* I am not and don't know how to be.

- I *should* have more money, *but* I am stuck in a dead-end job.

- I *should* lose weight, *but* I will start sometime soon.

- I *should* stop smoking, *but* I have tried before and failed.

See how you are building the perfect little trap for yourself by using this statement? You are blaming something outside of yourself, or relying on something outside of you to bring change. You're effectively denying personal responsibility.

Now, as a little experiment, look at the first "I should" list again and replace the word "should" with " want to," and see how it reads. The difference in your neurology will be noticeable.

"I want to" is a solution focused statement, whereas an "I should" statement will always be followed with "but". If there is something in particular you want out of life, it will never be obtained by using the words "I should".

Your mind, given half the chance and with some effort on your part, will give you what you want; whereas "should" will have the complete opposite effect. It will ensure you keep postponing whatever it is you think you should be doing. If you want something, then go out and try your best to get it. If you fall short, it's okay, that's being human. The path from wanting to getting is never straight.

> **Better to try something and falter than to never even start.**

As an interesting thought process you could do for the coming week, listen intently to your own language and also to the language of other people:

- Notice where you are saying "I should" and effectively stalling yourself from taking any action.

- Notice when other people are saying "you should," and educate yourself on the difference between information and manipulation.

- Listen to your own language, and start replacing the word "should" with "want" and see how that feels. You might decide you didn't want whatever *it* was in the first place; maybe *it* isn't worth the effort. Only you can decide.

- Give up using "I should" and beating yourself up for being weak. It serves no purpose other than to keep you stuck and going nowhere.

- Make an effort to remove "I should" from your vocabulary.

It takes a bit of forethought and practice to remove an established statement from your vocabulary, but it can be done. It just takes a bit of time

110

and attention, but the rewards will far outweigh the effort.

CHAPTER 15

Worrying About What Others Think

Are you concerned about what other people think of you? If you answered yes, then you are normal. If you answered no, then you are still normal, but you are playing a game of bravado. What a sneaky question. I have to say I feel very pleased with myself for thinking it up. Here's the thing, we are hardwired by evolution to be concerned about what people think of us. Notice I didn't say "worry" about what people think of us, as worry is a choice.

We gather information about ourselves and our environment by being concerned about what others think of us. It is a completely natural process and as much a part of you as your eye colour, and it cannot be turned off. "Not caring" what people think flies in the face of evolution and is a statement normally used by someone who actually does care what people think, they just don't want anyone to know it.

Which of these two statements carry the most power? Which one would you most like to live your life by?

- I don't *care* what people think of me.

- I won't be *defined* by what people think of me.

The first statement *looks* more attractive. It conjures up images of invincibility, and it feels like you have an invisible force field where the opinions of others don't matter as they just bounce off. The only problem with a force field is, while nothing can get in, you also can't get out.

"I don't *care* what people think of me" is a statement of bravado. You do actually care what others think of you, you just don't want anyone to know it. Another problem with having a force field is you eliminate connection with fellow human beings. How can I communicate with you, when you don't care what I think?

"I won't be *defined* by what people think of me" is a statement of fact; you don't need a false shield to protect you. Lines of communication are open; you get to decide what and who you want to believe. There is absolutely nothing wrong being concerned with what people think of you, but worrying about it is a completely different story.

I could at this point say something you have probably seen written in so many books, or that has been said to you, which is, "Don't worry what people think of you", or "You are being silly thinking this way". Brilliant—why didn't you think of this? Just ignore the problem, and it will go away.

113

Unfortunately, what is actually happening here is called "kinaesthetic denial". In other words, you temporarily *feel* better about the problem, but the problem still exists. It's like taking painkillers for a toothache. It feels good at the time, but the problem tooth is still there.

Anyone who advises not being concerned or accuses you of being silly either:

- Has never experienced the problem themselves, or

- Is showing profound ignorance of the problem

Either way we can discount those two pieces of sage advice.

How about getting a different perspective on what other people think of you? My intention is to get you thinking in a different way about a common problem we've all experienced. I could go into a diatribe about how we have evolved to judge and make assumptions to keep us alive, but I won't. Let's just say your evolution has ensured your survival by rendering you capable of making judgements and assumptions very quickly.

So why do we care what people think of us? We care because it triggers something we all have a problem with: the fear of rejection. We fit in, we conform, we know our place, all because of fear. We don't go on the date, write the book, follow our dreams, or step out of line. We stay in the comfort zone and lead an unfulfilled life because of what other people think of us, based on their standards of what we should be.

Read the last paragraph again, and then have a think about it for a few minutes.

Have I described your life? Does it sound "just like you"? If it does, then you are not alone. It's something most people struggle with. Tell everyone you're writing a book, and you will find out first-hand how it feels. I can speak from experience. But you don't have to write a book to find out. Just change what you are currently doing in your life.

People will be queuing up to tell you how silly you are, to tell you "you're not good enough", to tell you to "know your place". Sound familiar? There are various reasons why someone might do this, which we shall explore. Some people do it to hurt, some do it to protect, and others do it because you're making them feel uncomfortable.

If at any time when you're reading this chapter you feel insulted, then know it was done deliberately to get you thinking. I want to wake you up to reality with a few hard-hitting facts, and sometimes they will sting. So let me apologise in advance. No, actually I won't apologise, because if I did, it would mean I'm worried what you think of me—so how could I tell you not to worry about what other people think? Hmm ... deep.

So here goes with my first insulting fact: you are just not that important. Actually, that should read,

"You're just not that important to other people". People you love and care about think you're important, and their opinion of you should matter because it comes from a place of protection (usually). Those who know and love us have our best interests at heart most of the time. We can never say all of the time, because there will always be exceptions to the rule.

But if we constantly worry about what other people think of us—I mean people outside our circle of close family and friends—then we have an overblown sense of our own importance. Most people on this planet don't even know we exist, much less care about what we are doing.

> ➤ **They're not thinking about us; we're thinking about them.**

They are thinking about themselves and *their* lives one hundred percent of the time. We are so much inside our own heads we barely notice what is going on in the outside world. Unless it directly affects them, we barely register in the minds of most other people. We just *assume* we are in their thoughts.

Let me set up a scenario for you to prove this is true. President Barack Obama made a mistake by fluffing his lines during his oath-of-office speech. Can you tell me the exact point where it happened? Considering this was a truly historical event, you should have no problem remembering, right? It was broadcast around the world and seen by millions, if not billions, of people.

Can you see where this is going? If you can't remember a historical event seen by billions, then what are the chances of anyone remembering or caring what you do?

I can answer the question for you: no chance. Because we are not that important, we just think we are. Most people watching this historical event were probably thinking to themselves, "I wonder what's for lunch," or something similar. It's what we do. It's not because we don't care, it's because we are human. So the next time someone accuses you of not listening, you will know why you weren't.

Actually, we don't listen most of the time; we hear, but we don't listen. We are so much inside our own heads, and this is part of the problem. We are constantly listening to and acting on the little negative voice inside of us.

We listen to our negative thoughts as if they were reality, and the inner voice goes unchallenged, causing havoc in the background. If I said some of the things you say to yourself, you would punch me in the mouth, and what's more, I would deserve it. At the very least, you might challenge me as to why I think the way I do about you. You never consider challenging yourself, but all this is about to change.

Before we get to the actual technique of challenging your own thinking, I want to give you an example of making a wrong assumption. It will show how we distort our own thinking to make an assumption a reality. This is probably similar to what you do; actually, we all do it at some time.

A friend of mine called Nikki, who was into horseback riding, invited me to come along to observe a private lesson she was having. It took place in a typical large indoor arena. At one end there was a raised box where the instructor sat in an elevated position so he could observe the rider and give her instructions.

Anyhow, I was sitting in this box with the instructor watching my friend taking her lesson, and I have to say I was impressed. About forty-five minutes into the one-hour lesson, a group of five riders assembled underneath the box where I was seated. I could see them, but they couldn't see me.

All I could hear for the next fifteen minutes was the five riders talking about how good Nikki was and how good she was at controlling the horse. One of them even said, "I wish I could be as good as her." Let's just say the praise was coming thick and fast. Fifteen minutes later, Nikki and I were sitting in the box observing the same five riders having *their* lesson.

I will never forget what Nikki said next: "Those five riders are really good, aren't they? I wish I could control a horse like they can. I bet they thought I was terrible."

How wrong could she have been? She just displayed a perfect example of making an assumption and turning it into a reality, without challenging if her thinking was correct. Needless to say, I told her what *actually* happened and what they thought of her ability.

Obviously I have no idea what the riders we were now observing were thinking about Nikki watching them, but I wouldn't mind betting they were thinking, "I bet she thinks I'm terrible." We have no idea what a fellow human being is thinking about us, we just assume wrongly it has got to be negative. As you can see from the example, it just isn't true; we just make an assumption it is.

Someone gives us what we perceive to be a strange look, and we turn it into, "They must think I'm ugly (or weird or _____"). Fill in the blank. We can turn something said to us into something which means the complete opposite, and then worry about it non-stop.

> **We give meaning where no meaning exists, apart from inside our own heads.**

It is true there will be people who won't like you, won't like what you do, won't like how you dress, won't like how you speak. That's okay; we can't be all things to all people, all of the time. They are making a judgement of you based on their own internal filters and standards of how they think things should be.

We don't have to change what people think of us; we have to change the way we think about ourselves. It's impossible to stop people from thinking what they think, and impossible to stop them from making assumptions about us. Making assumptions is

119

hardwired into our DNA, so why would we even bother trying? All we can control is our reactions to our own thinking.

These people, whoever they are, are not thinking about us; we are thinking about them, and they don't care. We are engaged in a mind game of "Please like me", which we can't possibly win because we are the only player.

When we are worrying about what others think of us, we are engaged in automatic thinking. By "automatic thinking," I mean mind chatter ... thinking that runs by itself as if set on autopilot. If the automatic thinking goes unchallenged, our subconscious mind will accept the thought as true. You will then begin to display a behaviour that matches the thought.

For example: If your belief is, "If I spend money on myself, people will think I am selfish", then you will start to display a behaviour that matches your belief. You will start second guessing yourself every time you want or need to spend money. In the most extreme circumstances it is a real possibility this belief can be turned into, "If I spend money, then it makes me a bad person." You really don't want this for yourself.

All is not lost though. The fact you were not born with a set of beliefs means they can be challenged and changed.

We need to be able to jump straight in immediately after we have an automatic thought about what others think of us. We have to challenge the automatic thought as quickly as possible. We do this by asking ourselves two questions:

> **Is what I am thinking actually true?**

> **Can I prove it?**

Yes, it really is this simple, and I will explain how it works. "Is what I am thinking actually true?" brings the thought from the subconscious to the conscious mind, thus stopping automatic inner-critic thinking in its tracks. Now we have the thought in the conscious mind; we can decide if the thought equates with reality.

In many cases, once we become conscious of the automatic thought, we can plainly see that it is not true, or that it's only partially true. In either of these cases, simply revise and restate the problematic thought to yourself. The subconscious mind will hear the corrected version (particularly if you say it aloud), and will start to understand that's it's been telling you something false.

There are other times, though, when our answer to "Is what I am thinking actually true?" will be "Yes", or "I'm not sure". When this occurs, simply move on to the second question: "Can I prove it?" In most cases, you'll see the assumption is based on zero evidence.

In the "I'm selfish because I spend" example, you would have to prove to yourself that you are, in fact, actually selfish. You would need to review your life behaviours and interactions, asking yourself whether you make your choices with only you in mind or if you also do things for the good of others. I'm willing to bet a good deal of money that, for most of us, the review would show the selfishness charge is baseless. It is only based on an assumption of what other people think. Once you look at the evidence, the actual truth emerges.

Any self-critical mind chatter—and certainly any thoughts about what other people think— can be tackled with this technique. The technique's power is in the simplicity of the questions. There is nothing complicated about tackling automatic thinking. You just need to be aware you are doing it in the first place and then ask yourself the questions.

So, to recap:

- Come out from behind the "I don't care what people think" shield.

- Be concerned about—not defined by—what other people think.

- Don't give meaning where none exists.

Challenge self-critical automatic thoughts with the two reality-check questions.

From a personal perspective, the reality-check technique has helped me more times than I can remember. I use it on a regular basis if I get stuck in a negative thinking loop.

Hold on: you didn't think that because I wrote this book I don't experience times of negativity and insecurity, did you? I do, of course, and I'm not ashamed to admit it. I accept it as you should, as the price we sometimes have to pay for being human.

Before you turn the page to start the next chapter, take a minute and have a go at the reality-check technique. Think about something in your recent past where you worried what people thought of you, and then ask yourself the two questions.

CHAPTER 16

Believe in Yourself

What we believe about ourselves can cause us all kinds of problems or—if the belief is positive—can actually smooth our path through life. But I'm not going to tell you to "just believe in yourself and all your problems will be over". That would be an oversimplification of how things work. Instead I'm going to share with you how to change a belief you currently hold about yourself.

Even if you have a positive self-image, there will be a few things about yourself you believe to be true that you would like to change. This chapter will explain how.

Beliefs play such a powerful part in our lives. We weren't born with them, but we sometimes live as if they are eternal and unchangeable. In actual fact, the opposite is true. Beliefs are what make you the person you are, good or bad. They shape your very essence and control what you do. They are invisible, but powerful. Beliefs can bring you to your knees or enable you to reach the highest achievements possible.

So what do *you* believe? Henry Ford once said, "Whether you think you can or you think you can't, you're right." If you replace the word *think* with the word *believe,* his meaning becomes even clearer. Put simply:

> ➤ **You are what you believe yourself to be.**

If you believe you have high self-esteem, you're right. If you believe you have low self-esteem, you're right. The belief creates the reality.

Here's the thing: you weren't born with beliefs. A belief is only an idea you have taken on, not something carved into stone. A belief can be changed, moulded, or dropped altogether. If you think this isn't true, let me ask you a couple of questions. Do you believe in something today which you didn't believe in ten years ago? Have you dropped a belief about yourself that you once held to be true? If you answered yes to either of those questions, where did the belief go? Can you see it was just an idea you held and that idea can be changed?

Most of us carry around so many negative beliefs about ourselves, it's a wonder we don't collapse under the weight. We carry our labels like a stone around our neck, forever there, forever holding us back. Some of these labels might be:

- I'm stupid.

- I'm no good.

- I'm a depressive.

125

- I'm useless.

- I'm old.

- I'm ugly.

- [Put your favourite label here]

If you look closely, all the above statements are about our identity. Beliefs about who we are as a person.

When we whisper bad messages about ourselves to ourselves, we look to our environment for evidence to support the statement. If it appears we have found it, we then start to become that statement. We will start living as if we are stupid, no good, ugly, or whatever. Henry Ford's quote makes a bit more sense now, doesn't it?

Let's shift gears for a moment, because I want to describe for you a psychological phenomenon known as *priming*. Have you ever had this experience? There's something out there you want, and you can't get your mind off it. You seem to spend every waking second thinking about it—a bit of an exaggeration, I know, but you get the point. Now comes the strange part: you notice the very thing you have been thinking about turning up in your environment. I don't think there is a human being who hasn't experienced this.

Let's use online shopping as an example of what I mean.

Have you ever had the experience of trying to source something online, only to realise that it seems very difficult to find? A day or two of searching and you eventually find what you have been looking for on some obscure website. You purchase said item, and then what happens? That's right, you start seeing advertisements everywhere for the item you just purchased. Just to add insult to injury, it's normally cheaper as well.

Television advertising uses this to great effect. Have you ever wondered why you keep seeing the same advertisement over and over again? Advertisers know your subconscious mind learns by repetition. They also know what they show you onscreen repeatedly, you'll start to notice in your environment. For instance, there may be a new cereal product that ordinarily you would not notice in the display of dozens of cereals in the supermarket. But because they've saturated you with so many images of this cereal, next time you go to the store, the box jumps right out at you from all the others in the category. You've remembered the advertisement and bang, your brain makes the association. You buy the product, take it home, then wonder why you bought it in the first place. It's not your fault; you just became the victim of a clever marketing ploy.

The above example is pretty harmless because most of the time we know we have been had. Who wouldn't want to sample those delicious-looking chocolate biscuits, the ones with the foil wrapper, they just look so …Hold on a minute, that was about me. Delete this last paragraph from your mind.

The real danger from priming comes when we *aren't* aware—especially when what we're seeing in the environment reinforces a negative belief about ourselves. Whether the belief is positive or negative, then just like in the cereal-box example, we'll start noticing things around us that seem to match our belief.

Have you ever noticed when you're feeling down, everything and everybody seems to get on your nerves? You have primed yourself by thinking negative thoughts to notice everything which is negative in your environment, which in turn reinforces your feelings of depression. It works exactly the same way if you think of yourself as stupid or no good. You'll notice yourself being what you consider stupid or no good, and seeing that will strengthen the negative opinion you hold of yourself. It's kind of like the old saying: "Give a dog a bad name, and you'll have a bad dog."

Now multiply this by a week, a month, a year, and before we know it, the negative self-belief has become a habit. A habit that keeps on reinforcing itself. At this point you will also be displaying the behaviours that support the negative belief about yourself. All of this is happening outside of your conscious awareness, which is the problem. But not for much longer.

Sometimes it can be difficult to persuade yourself to get rid of an old belief you have held for so long; it's like an old coat you don't want to throw away. It's been around so long you have gotten used to it, you've grown into it. But throw it away you must, because it's restricting your growth as a human being. It is keeping you scared and in your comfort zone. Your inner critic may start telling you, "This is going to be tough." But guess what? You can decide it's going to be fun.

Did you ever dream of being an actor? I'll bet at some point in your past you did. We all have a little actor inside us, just wanting to get out. Well, now it's going to get its chance. The technique I'm going to teach you requires you to pretend to be an actor, and the "audience" is going to be your own subconscious mind. You, with your brilliant Hollywood performance, are going to fool your subconscious into believing something new and different about yourself. Acting is required, and also a leap of faith. Does that sound like fun? Perhaps we'll even nominate you for an Oscar. Here's how this little technique works.

The subconscious mind learns by repetition, and we can use this learning ability to instil a new belief, one more beneficial to you. This is where the acting comes in. For the sake of example, let's say the belief you want to change is "I have no self-confidence." You want to change it to: "I am self-confident." This is just an example, and you can substitute whatever belief you want to change as the process is exactly the same. So if you are ready, let's go. It might help if you close your eyes when doing this process.

I want you to imagine what a self-confident person looks like. (Confident is just the book example—I actually want you to insert the belief you

129

are hoping to develop. If you want to be more patient, I want you to imagine what a patient person looks like. If you want to be happier, then imagine what a happy person looks like. Get it? Got it. Good.)

So back to the example ... How does a self-confident person carry themselves? What do they look like? What sort of clothes do they wear? How do they speak? Really get into imagining the fine details.

Imagine how it would feel for *you* to be very self-confident. What sensations would you be feeling in your body? What would your inner voice sound like? What's it like to feel calm and in control?

If you allow your imagination to really run with this process, you will experience what it is like to be confident, if only for a few moments. The important thing is your subconscious mind wasn't able to tell the difference between you *imagining* you were confident and you actually *being* confident. The result is, you tricked your subconscious. It is starting to change its opinion of you. It's starting to regard you as confident. The inner critic has been fooled, and every time you do this exercise, the message will get through to your subconscious more strongly: "I am a self-confident person."

I want you to do this exercise several times today. Do it where you won't be interrupted or distracted. You will probably notice you're able to keep the confident feeling longer and longer each time you do this exercise. You are priming your subconscious mind to accept a new way of thinking. Remember: it doesn't

130

know the difference between fantasy and reality. That's why you wake up in a cold sweat after a vivid dream.

By repeating this exercise several times a day, you will soon not only be *feeling* self-confident, you will be *acting* self-confident. It's only a short distance to *becoming* self-confident, but you have to be prepared to step out of your comfort zone to get into the "becoming" territory. It is necessary to get comfortable with feeling uncomfortable; there are no shortcuts to this part. You can read a hundred books on self-confidence, and they will all suggest this next step.

You start out small. You pick a situation from real life that will push you slightly out of your comfort zone, but that won't have you breaking out into a cold sweat just thinking about it. I will tell you exactly what I did when I went through this next step in the process.

I used to have a problem walking up to a group of people and getting involved in their conversation. I did the imagining exercise I described, over and over for several days. This allowed me to have the feeling of how it would be to mingle naturally in a social situation. The next step was to practice the skill in the real world. I began small, by practicing stepping into a conversation with two people I knew reasonably well. The voice inside my head was saying, "Don't do it, don't do it!" But another voice was saying, "If I don't do it now, I never will."

Now here's the important bit. I walked over to them and acted *as if* I was confident, just like how I had imagined it so many times before. I *knew* I was

131

acting. I was faking it. I was playing a part, and if my knees were knocking—and they were—no one noticed or cared. I repeated this process over and over and over again, with bigger and more challenging social groups, until it became second nature. Pretty soon I really *was* confident. I was play-acting no longer. I didn't fake it until I made it. I faked it until I *became* it. So can you.

Today it wouldn't cost me a thought to walk up to a group of people I didn't know well and get involved. You can do exactly the same, but you have to be prepared to take setbacks. You will have to fight your own temptation to give up and take the easy option of doing nothing. You, too, can fake it until you become it. Don't put up with a lifetime of self-imposed restriction. It is a lot easier to change a behaviour than to change a belief. The strange thing is, when you change the behaviour (through imagining and play-acting), then a change of belief automatically follows. All you need to do then is to practice to keep the new belief in place.

If I were in your position right now, I would be saying to myself, "It can't be this easy." Remarkably, it is, but you have to test the technique to know that for yourself. If you remember how the subconscious mind works, you know it rejects any attempt at change unless the change is gradual and the process is repeated. That means you need to keep repeating the imagining and play-acting in order to get the desired results.

Don't be in a hurry. It's not a race. You have the rest of your life to feel great about your new belief. I can't emphasise enough the need for practice. You are learning a new skill, and like any skill it needs to be honed and adapted to suit not only your needs, but also your lifestyle. You will have to come up with creative ways to expand your boundaries and move beyond your current limitations.

Believe me: you can do this. Remember, the process isn't about telling yourself *you are* confident, it's about acting *as if* you are confident. Congratulate yourself when things go as planned. Use any setbacks as feedback that your process requires a little tweak here and there. If you feel the endeavour is a bit daunting, that's a normal reaction and not a sign of weakness. The fact that you are willing to give it a go is a sign of strength and should be applauded. Imagine some time in the future, and you're looking back at how far you've come. Surely that vision is worth a bit of challenge and effort. Imagine how much it could potentially change your life for the better.

The process I have given you will work on the vast majority of beliefs. I'm not arrogant enough to think it will work with everyone and with everything all of the time. You will have to try it to find out for yourself. Adapt it, play with it, change whatever needs changing to suit your purposes, but most importantly practice it. And when you get bored, practice it some more. I think you will be pleasantly surprised with the results. How long does it take? As long as you need to make the change you desire. We're all so different that it's impossible to put a time frame on the process.

Sometimes—depending on the belief you want to eliminate or install—a further step has to be taken. For instance, if the belief is you feel stupid and the new belief centres around feeling intelligent, you might want to read a few books on communication techniques or assertiveness. It's impossible to predict what steps you might be inspired to take, but if something positive occurs to you, go with it. Listen to the positive messages from your subconscious mind, and let them guide you to a better future.

CHAPTER 17

Mistakes Are There to Be Made

I have a question for you. What is the quickest way to lose friends and alienate people? By pointing out their mistakes. It is a very human and tempting thing to do, as we think we are helping the other person, but this is rarely the case.

This is something I have to admit to being guilty of myself: pointing out another person's mistakes for no apparent reason other than maybe to feel better about myself. I am glad to say I rarely do it these days. I literally trained it out of myself, and so can you. Why did I want to train it out of myself? Surely I only gave my sage advice to prevent other people from doing something wrong?

Well, I could give myself that excuse and just keep performing the behaviour, but that would be a lie. The simple fact is, if we're pointing out another person's errors and not giving them a solution, then we're talking just for the sake of it. There is even more to it than this. We are also training ourselves to keep a look out for everything negative. If this isn't bad

135

enough, we are also telling the other person, "You're not good enough".

> **The good news is: we didn't do it deliberately. The bad news is, now that we're aware, and we continue doing it, we *are* doing it deliberately.**

Is there anything useful to be gained by making someone feel they are not good enough? I don't think so. But that's exactly what's happening when we point out a mistake and leave it at that. If we were to point out a mistake and then help to supply a solution, that's a different story.

Pointing out a mistake is a bit like a double-edged sword; it cuts in both directions. It cuts the first party because they start doubting their own ability, and it cuts our direction because we are priming ourselves to only pay attention to negativity. We also get another cut from the sword, because if we're focused on negativity then *we* start to feel *we* are not good enough, and around and around it goes, spiralling downward.

We're certainly very complicated, aren't we? Fortunately there is an antidote—if we can help the other person find a solution to the mistake they made, then the whole process is reversed.

Most people know when they have made a mistake. What they don't need is their nose rubbed in it just for good measure. Put yourself in the other person's position, and imagine how it feels for them. Become aware of other people's feelings before you're tempted to walk all over them. It might be your turn next.

Speaking of mistakes ... what about those times when *you* make mistakes? Well, it's not the end of the world. As human beings we constantly strive to become bigger than ourselves; just think how technology has evolved in the last twenty years. If we are evolving, then inevitably mistakes will be made. It's how we learn. But somehow we have managed to turn a valuable learning experience into something which should be avoided at all costs.

Making a mistake has become something we should be ashamed of. It's this way because of conditioning. We were taught to get things right and never admit to failure, as that could be seen as a sign of weakness to be exploited. We have managed to turn trivial mistakes into judgemental reflections on ourselves personally.

Admit your mistakes, if only to yourself. Admit that yes, you're human, and yes, you make them. It's not necessary to take out a full-page advertisement in a national newspaper; a quiet internal reflection will suffice. There is absolutely no need to use making a mistake as an excuse to start beating yourself up.

Probably one of the most televised mistakes of all time was the incident we talked about earlier, when American President Barack Obama fluffed his lines during his oath-of-office speech, and he did it in front of millions. Do you honestly think he sat in the Oval

137

Office afterwards wringing his hands with regret and worry?

"I always make mistakes". Be careful if you're telling yourself that on a regular basis. The subconscious mind has a nasty habit of giving you what you focus on.

If your focus is on negativity and how you always make mistakes, the inner critic will look to your environment for proof to support your belief. It will have no trouble finding evidence, as you have primed yourself to look for it. Now you are in the territory of a self-fulfilling prophesy, and your behaviour will now match your belief. Scary!

There is an easy way to counteract all of the above. Just tell yourself you are human and admit to your mistakes as they happen, then move on. Initially it can be a bit difficult changing this habit, but with a little honest reflection, you will be able to do it. The hardest part will be taking responsibility for your own errors. No one really likes admitting they are wrong. With practice, you can achieve maximum benefit from this technique. It might also help you think twice before pointing out someone else's mistakes.

Hindsight is great, isn't it? It allows us to beat ourselves up over something that was merely an error of judgement based on our knowledge at the time. We can only see a mistake in retrospect; we are looking backwards with the benefit of hindsight, and then punishing ourselves for making the wrong choice. We're playing a mind-reading game with ourselves.

The best choice we could make was made at the time, based on our knowledge *at* the time. We are now making a judgement of our past based on today's new knowledge. That's not very fair, is it?

Think of it this way: If we could go back to the time we made the mistake, with only the knowledge we possessed at the time, would we make the same mistake? Yes, we would, because we didn't have the knowledge we now have in the present. So why do we need to berate ourselves? Unless of course we enjoy playing the role of victim. Unfortunately, some people do.

What about those times when we knew better and made the mistake anyhow?

I can't deny it, this would be a tough pill to swallow, especially if our actions caused harm to another human being. If you remember back at the introduction, I said that we are a contradiction ruled by emotions and feelings. Well this is one of those instances that emotions or feelings can overrule logic. Sometimes we just do things for no apparent reason. It doesn't make sense, but it is an aspect of being human. To avoid such instances we would need the ability to predict the future consequences of our actions or inactions. It might help to move away from the *why* of what happened and instead focus on *what* are we going to do to prevent it from happening in the future. Unfortunately the past cannot be undone, we can only change our reaction to it.

To never make mistakes is to be a perfect human being. So unless you are perfect, it's time to move on and realise you cannot change the past. A mistake will always be a mistake, regardless of how much we would like the opposite to be true.

Can we take responsibility for our mistakes and move on? Of course we can, but it requires us to make a choice to do so. Sometimes we do nothing, because it is the easy option. There is a slight problem with this mindset: it will keep us stuck, and will also promote a feeling of not being good enough.

A mistake is a learning experience that we can use for our benefit or ignore. Sometimes the mistake is costly, but there is always something to be learned. There is *always* something we could do differently in the future—something we would have done differently in the past, had we but known.

Can you put the mistake right, or do you need to accept that it happened and move on? If you can set things right through some words or actions, by all means, do so. If you cannot, learn from the experience and get past it. Accepting we did something wrong can be difficult, but it's no harder than torturing yourself over something you can do nothing about.

As human beings, we are designed to make mistakes. It literally is how we evolved. Our conscious and subconscious minds are in constant debate when a decision has to be made. Is it any wonder that sometimes we get it wrong? Take it easy on yourself when you mess up. It happens. Naturally we would prefer that it didn't, but this would require you being able to go backwards in time and predict the future. Oh, how I wish I could do some time travelling myself to set certain things right, but then if I did, you wouldn't be reading this book. I wouldn't have written this book and maybe I would cease to exist, and then maybe … hold on, I need go lie down in a darkened room. See you in the next chapter.

CHAPTER 18

Perfectionism in an Imperfect World

Have you ever met someone who was either a genius or a great inspiration, someone you just knew, if they applied themselves, would be unstoppable? I met such a person in my therapy practice. Anna came to me for help with what she thought was a problem with procrastination.

Anna would start projects, but never saw them through to the end. Which was a pity, as she was the sort of person who could probably take a stick of chewing gum and a thumb tack and then make a business out of it. She just couldn't seem to get to the next level, but didn't understand why.

After we had a long conversation, a pattern in her behaviour started to emerge. Anna would start a project, get three or four weeks in, and then, in her words, "get distracted with something totally irrelevant". Her last project was an innovation I won't talk about lest someone decides to steal her idea. Let's just say this innovation would make her some serious money.

142

She started the project, and everything was looking great. Then suddenly, out of nowhere, she developed an overpowering interest in restoring vintage furniture. This pattern had been repeated many times in her life, and she wanted to know why.

It turned out Anna had two issues—perfectionism and a fear of failure—which were both feeding off of each other. Her fear of failure was actually a fear of being judged, and her perfectionism was a way of not being judged, or so she thought. Her own mind was sabotaging her. No, actually, she was sabotaging herself. If she didn't finish a project, then she couldn't be judged. If she worked perfectly, then (in her mind) people wouldn't judge her. Around and around it went in a never-ending circle.

How does this story apply to you? Perfectionism, on the face of it, is a noble virtue to pursue. After all, who wouldn't like to be perfect? There is only one slight little problem with this way of thinking. By virtue of the fact that you're human, it follows you cannot be perfect, no matter how hard you try.

Perfectionism can affect our lives in lots of damaging ways. Later I will give you some solutions to overcome perfectionism, but for now just realise it's not something you were born with and not something you inherited. It's just a learned behaviour that can just as easily be unlearned.

What became of Anna? I would really like to tell you she is now a multimillionaire and claim all the credit, but that wouldn't be true. I can tell you, though, she is happier than she has ever been in her life, now that she knows why she does what she does. She feels like she is more of a success than ever before. We all have our own ways of defining success, and they aren't always purely financial.

Strange how we are living at a time in history when we literally have the world at our fingertips. The internet, mobile phones, twenty-four-hour everything and instant most things. Yet for all of this, we are at a time in history when we are the unhappiest we've ever been. We self-medicate with food, alcohol, drugs, and just about anything we can use to silence the voice of our inner critic, which tells us incessantly, "You're not good enough." Our inner critic is having a great time because we don't have the perfect life, and it likes to remind us so on a regular basis.

It doesn't help when we are also fed a continual diet of guilt and shame that our lives are not filled with the ultimate happiness, the ultimate self-confidence, and so on. Is it any wonder depression is on the rise, and we feel enough is *never* enough? If there is a human trait guaranteed to trigger feelings of not being good enough, then striving for perfection has got to be it. Perfectionism is like an acid eating away at your very core. At first glance, it looks like something that could be useful, until you realise too late it's dominating your life.

What must it be like to be perfect? Thankfully, it's not something I will have to worry about, judging by what looks back at me from the mirror.

The sad thing is, even someone you regard as being or looking perfect is not perfect. You just think that they are, based on your own internal assumptions and judgements. Perfection is an impossible dream to achieve, but why is it so?

As humans we are goal-driven, which means once we achieve a certain standard, we are driven by our own evolution to go beyond it. If perfection is your goal, then it flies in the face of your own evolution because perfection means you have reached the end, you have made it, there is nowhere else left to go. This doesn't make a lot of sense because if you are at the end it means you're not susceptible to evolution driving you to achieve a yet higher standard and a yet higher level of perfection. Perfectionism is like being in a room with no doors. Your only option is to go around in circles. It's a self-made prison sentence with no chance of parole.

Let's take a look at an example of how damaging striving for perfection can be. The media, advertising, and film industries would have every man and woman on the planet believe what is depicted is the "ideal", and if *you* are not the "ideal" then *you* are somehow lacking. We are the wrong height, wrong weight, have the wrong bone structure, wrong everything.

I suppose the fact that a multibillion-dollar industry has evolved around getting us to believe we

145

are lacking is a mere coincidence; maybe the models and actors do actually look in real life like they do in the pictures and films. Maybe there isn't an army of computer geeks airbrushing out all the pimples, wrinkles, and imperfections to sell us something that in real life is impossible to achieve and does not exist.

It certainly sells cars, hair products, cosmetics, aftershave, etc. The list is endless, and all based on the premise that we're lacking. We are very small cogs in a machine designed to relieve us of our money. We are all supposed to crave the "ideal", but here is where the problem lies: you can only ever be you; there is no other human being on Earth like you. Even an identical twin brought up in the same household is not you. Their life experience will be completely different from yours.

There is something in our neurology: a little program that runs at a subconscious level. We might not be aware of it, but the advertising industry certainly is and exploits it ruthlessly. For ease of understanding, we will call this "the comparisons program". It probably has a fancier title, but I don't know it, and you don't care. Anyhow, the comparisons program is hardwired by evolution into every aspect of your life. A hardwired evolutionary program is normally in place inside our minds to ensure survival of the species—in other words, you. So we need to go a bit further back in time to understand why it is there and what it does.

Imagine the scene. We are a caveman/woman sitting happily in our cave when we find out our next-door neighbour has discovered fire and a more efficient club for dispatching tonight's meal. Instantly our comparisons program kicks in, and we think, "If we don't get what they have, our survival will be threatened." So we get our fire and our shiny new club and thus ensure our evolution. What would have happened if we had sat in our caves and thought, "I will go looking for fire and a new club when I have the time." We would have probably ceased to exist.

I hope you realise from my brief explanation of the comparisons program that there's a lot more to it than this, but my name isn't Darwin, and I don't want you to die of boredom, so we shall continue.

Now fast forward a few thousand generations to the present day. Although we look reasonably civilised, the same little program is still there running in the background, waiting to be exploited. All I need to do now is activate the program in you, but how will I do that?

Easy. I simply need to show you something you don't have, and make it visually stimulating by giving you an impossibly attractive image of a person or a thing. I encourage a sense of lack, and presto! I am inside your program.

We want what they have, but how to get it? Well, we just buy whatever it is they are selling, and we can be like them. The problem is, you are not them. They are not even themselves. They are an airbrushed, polished, computer-generated version of someone else's vision of the "ideal", but the program is up and

147

running. It's driving us to obtain what *they* have. Even though we know logically we are falling for it, we still do it because the program is running in an illogical part of the mind, that doesn't listen to rational argument. This is why we buy with emotion and then justify with reason.

We are processing, "If only I could get *that*, I would feel so much better". So we buy into the dream, and guess what? It doesn't deliver on the promise. We don't feel any better; as a matter of fact, we feel worse for falling for the unobtainable perfect dream ... again. So now we really *do* need to make ourselves feel better. How? Well, by buying into another unobtainable dream, of course! And so the cycle continues, while the advertisers laugh all the way to the bank.

Does all this sound painfully familiar? I hope it does and makes you want to break this cycle of cynical manipulation. Why does all this matter? For one thing, because people all over the world are dying of anorexia and bulimia chasing the *ideal* body. For another, because people all over the world are getting into a lifetime of debt they can never repay. All in pursuit of something that does not exist in the real world.

Do we really want to conform to what someone else tells us we should be—especially when that someone is an industry motivated by profit and greed? If we are constantly making comparisons with impossible standards, can we ever feel happy or content? Can we ever silence the inner critic? I think you already know the answer. Accepting the fact that we are less than perfect is a very comfortable and safe place to exist. Your comparison program is there to ensure your survival. It's not there for manipulation by society or a need to conform to something you are not and can never be.

If you are on the comparisons treadmill, then you have nowhere to go. You can never reach perfection because it does not exist. Society, advertising, and a need to fit in are making you think this way. It's time to start thinking for yourself.

Here is a little thought which might help you off the treadmill: if you are not in control of your life and not thinking for yourself, then someone is doing the thinking for you and at the same time controlling you. Isn't that scary? I don't know about you, but it isn't the life I would choose.

Now that we've covered perfectionism inflicted upon us by others, let me introduce a not-so-obvious but equally damaging form of perfectionism we inflict upon ourselves. Here are a few examples of this more subtle form of perfectionism:

- Having to be *the best* at work.

- Having your children live up to *your* impossibly high standards.

- Having to have the *perfect* marriage, family, and/or relationships.

- Never admitting *you* are wrong.

149

Good enough is never good enough for you. Something that *has* been completed always feels like unfinished business; it could always have been better. Never perfect, somehow lacking.

Have you spotted the connection yet? Your happiness depends on other people falling into line with what *you* think constitutes perfection. Does this sound like a good strategy? If you answered yes, then you are beyond the scope of this book. But if you answered no, then keep reading.

Is this chapter hitting a nerve? We need to become aware of our never-ending quest to obtain the unobtainable. If we recognise the pattern, we can eliminate it. Can we stop being perfectionists? Yes, but a hard choice has to made. Is it what you really want? Or are you happy in your self-made prison? Some people are happy to continue on their path. They've been doing it so long it is now part of their identity. You will hear them say, "I am a perfectionist" and wear the badge with pride.

➤ **Perfectionism is a learned behaviour which can be unlearned; you weren't born with it.**

• Self-awareness is the key to ridding yourself of this particular waste of time once and for all; we need to become aware of our own automatic reactions. Once we become aware, we need to take a step back from those things that are keeping us in the prison. We have to:

• Let close enough be good enough

- Take our focus off perfect outcomes

- Realise and get comfortable with the concept of not being perfect

- Stop expecting other people to live up to our standards

- Stop wasting our time comparing ourselves to others

This will require a degree of concentrated self-reflection on your part, and then a willingness to let go of your learned behaviour. It will be as easy or as difficult as you expect it to be, but the journey will ultimately be worth it. Think about this sentence:

> **If we do nothing today, we can look forward to more of the same tomorrow.**

CHAPTER 19

Guilt

Wouldn't it be great if there was a technique that could take away the feelings of guilt we all experience from time to time? You know the ones, they go something like, "I wish I hadn't said/done that." Well it's your lucky day as I happen to have just the technique to quieten that critical inner voice.

Before we begin, a little word of warning: The technique generally doesn't work with the really big stuff. The instances where you know you did wrong, but just want to feel better about doing wrong. The sort of things like robbing a bank or telling your wife you actually enjoyed watching the film *The Mummy* for the hundredth time (oh, the shame of it). It's meant for the day to day type of guilt that just seems to niggle away at us in the background. By the way, there is a subtle difference between guilt and shame, which although feel the same are completely different.

- Guilt is when we feel like we did something bad.
- Shame is when we feel we are a bad person.

152

Guilt is about a feeling, whereas shame is about us personally. It might help to think of shame as guilt on steroids. It's important to recognise the distinction as shame is generally only resolved by talking to someone about it, preferably a professional.

The following process is best carried out with the eyes closed as it helps cut out any distractions. It shouldn't really take any more than two or three minutes at most.

Let's get to the technique:

1) Bring to mind the memory or event that caused your feelings of guilt. Now rate the feelings of guilt on a scale from one to ten, one being very mild guilt and ten being the most painful. Be very specific with the number, seven and a quarter is not being specific, whereas seven or eight is.

2) Let your mind drift back to a time before the guilt-producing incident, a time where you felt no guilt whatsoever. It might be the day before; it could even be a month or a year before the event. The time isn't important, what is important is the absence of feelings of guilt in the time you chose.

3) Stay with that feeling of absence of guilt for about thirty seconds.

4) This bit is really important, so sit up and stop slouching. Don't have me come back there.

Bringing the feelings of absence of guilt with you, drift forward in time to the guilt-producing incident and stop there for about ten seconds.

5) Drift forward in time and remember something you did this morning. Eating your breakfast, brushing your teeth, anything as long as it is in the here and now. Stay with the memory for about ten seconds.

6) Would have been to open your eyes, but if your eyes are not open, then how are you reading about opening your eyes?

Now, once again rate your feelings of guilt on a scale between one and ten. The feelings of guilt should now be reduced. If you want to reduce them further, just repeat the process until you are at a level you are comfortable with.

If the feelings of guilt have not reduced, this can be for a variety of easily corrected reasons:

1) The process requires repeating several times.

2) You didn't drift far enough back in time to where you experienced zero guilt.

3) You didn't drift forward into the present day, in the here and now.

4) It isn't guilt you are feeling, but shame instead.

If possible and applicable get someone to talk you through the process, you will probably find you have missed a step. If it isn't appropriate to have someone help you, then read the process a few times until you can memorise it.

Guilt is one of those emotions which serves no useful purpose. It isn't an evolutionary protection mechanism like fear, it's just something we learned and reinforced from a very young age. Guilt can very easily convert to shame if left unattended. It can convert from something we did to someone we are.

Now you have a technique to stop it from going that far.

Give the process a good trial on a regular basis to reap the maximum benefit. Don't be fooled by its simplicity, it's powerful for that exact reason – it is so simple. A process doesn't need to be long and complicated to be effective; it does however need to be repeated.

Now, if I could just find a way to wean my wife off *The Mummy*, my life would be free from guilt as well. Actually I know why she watches it so much, she has a thing for Oded Fehr, but we will keep that secret between you and me.

CHAPTER 20

Who Said Life Was Fair?

How did you feel when you read the title of this chapter? Did you feel like it meant you should just give in? Did you change it in your own mind to read, "Life's not worth living"? It was not my intention to give you that impression. Rather, I'm proposing that we embrace the fact that sometimes life *isn't* fair, so we may experience a new sense of freedom that always expecting life to be fair can never give us.

Sometimes bad things happen to good people … period. Unfortunately this includes you and me. When we live a life expecting everything to be fair, we are denying reality. It's a fantasy that only exists inside our heads. When we live like life *should* be fair, then we are devastated when it isn't. We look for answers which don't exist. We are perpetually stuck in a loop of "Why me?" or "What have I done to deserve this?" And the answers aren't coming anytime soon.

When we adopt an attitude of life not being fair, we will be able to handle whatever comes our way because now we will be looking for solutions.

The opposite is true when we think life *should* be fair. We will look instead for an answer which doesn't exist in the real world. Imagine life as a pendulum. As you know, a pendulum swings both ways. When life is good, you think to yourself, "Life is fair". Then you're surprised when the pendulum swings the other way and things are bad. Do you think this is realistic?

Do you think I'm being *pessimistic* and that we should always look on the bright side? I'm being *realistic* in an attempt to help you see life from a more workable perspective. But if constantly looking on the bright side is working for you, then by all means continue. The pendulum never swings in one direction; it normally comes the opposite direction when you least expect it. Why not be ready for it when it does?

> **You will never have to ask "Why me?" ever again; you will never have to ask "What have I done to deserve this?" because you will know sometimes *life's not fair.***

No amount of positive thinking will have any impact on these questions, because all we are doing when thinking positive is playing a game of kinaesthetic denial. In other words, we are making ourselves *feel* better about the problem and doing nothing to solve it. When you adopt an attitude of "sometimes life's not fair", the questions don't need answered because it is what it is. Bad events happen. It's not the event that's the main problem, it's our reaction to it. Of course, it's very tempting to sit back and do nothing when problems arrive, but all this does is create even more problems.

157

Life's not fair for all of us. (all this time and you thought life was only unfair to you.) We all have had times when we wished things could have turned out differently. That's not about life being fair, that's about you being human. Life not being fair isn't something I made up, it's an absolute fact of our human existence; we cannot ignore it and hope it will go away.

When you live life thinking life *should be* fair, then certain things are going to happen. You're fighting against yourself, and eventually it's going to exhaust you. Let me give you an example.

Let's say a person is involved in a car crash. Their leg gets broken and they are incapacitated for a while. Long enough to start thinking, "Why me?" Let's also say this person has a "life *should be* fair" attitude. What do you think will happen next? Well, they have an internal rule that says life should be fair, and that rule has just been broken. They know they didn't deserve this. So because a law of the universe seems to have been broken, the person feels cheated and punished. They droop and become unhappy. Soon they are feeling frustrated, angry, and maybe even depressed. They become difficult to live with.

Why is all this going on? Because they now have an internal conflict. They think things *should be* a certain way (fair), and their rebellious attitude is their mind's attempt at restoring order.

On the other hand, when you have an attitude that life sometimes is not fair, all this anguish can be avoided. You will see the accident as having no
158

meaning other than that you were in the wrong place at the wrong time. It's just one of those things; you accept it and move on. Does this mean you like what happened to you? No, but you can accept it as part of life not being fair. Sometimes bad things just happen. No part of this is about denial, but it is about being realistic.

Whenever we have a "life *should be* fair" attitude, it can very easily descend into a victim mindset, a "life is out to get me" way of thinking. That can descend even further into the likes of depression … and that's not what you want for yourself.

- Is it fair that people commit criminal acts and walk away without consequence? No.

- Is it fair that underserving people win large amounts of money? No.

- Is it fair that your past resembles a train wreck? No.

No, it isn't fair. But it is life, and sometimes life just happens.

Would it help you if you adopted an attitude of "sometimes life's not fair"? It might, but there's only one way to actually find out: trying it for yourself. Have a think about something in the past which didn't seem to have any reasonable explanation. Now apply the "sometimes life's not fair" attitude to it, and see what happens. Be aware if it has any effect on your way of thinking.

Most of the time you will notice a lightness and feel a different perspective around the issue, because your mind is not in conflict. It now sees the issue for what it was, something that happened outside of your control. If, on the other hand, you feel the need to fix the issue which you had no control over, then this is about you not accepting the fact that in this instance you were powerless to do anything. Reading the chapter on acceptance might prove helpful.

Some people may find this process particularly difficult, as they have invested so much time thinking things should be the way they *want* them to be. Sometimes it's hard to let go of a well-established way of thinking, even when we know it's doing harm. But maybe, just maybe, this might help you to get a different perspective on something that's been troubling you for far too long. Try it and see; give it the attention it deserves. All you have to lose is a lifetime of aggravation.

I'm going to end this chapter with a little challenge in the form of a question: where in your life, if you adopted an attitude of "sometimes life's not fair", would it have the most profound effect?

This is a short question which requires quite a bit of introspection to answer honestly, especially if you have lived a life thinking life *should be* fair. When you come up with some honest answers, try living the "sometimes life's not fair" attitude for a week and see what happens. There's every chance you'll start enjoying the type of freedom from restrictive thinking it gives you.

Notice if you have some internal resistance to doing this process. That's just your inner critic wanting things to stay the same. The resistance will soon disappear when you get into the swing of things. Who knows, you might even start enjoying having control over your own thought processes. I can certainly speak from experience and tell you it is very empowering. I have been there, done that, and felt the freedom. So can you. Enough said.

CHAPTER 21

Feeling Pissed Off Is Okay

You know the feeling. You have only woken up, and already you know it's going to be one of those days. You're just not yourself. You feel down in the dumps and are generally at war with everybody and everything—with yourself especially.

To add to your already mounting misery, everybody is telling you to cheer up and pull yourself together as you have so much to be thankful for. Wow, why didn't you think of that? All your problems would be over, and you wouldn't have to feel down.

Hooray! Join the club. You're human after all. You probably think you're the exception, and all this stuff only happens to you. That's okay. It just feels this way for now.

People in general are well-meaning. They may genuinely want to help you feel better, or they could be just fed up looking at your miserable face. Either way you feel their comments are about as useful as a chocolate teapot (mmm, chocolate). We have accepted we are feeling down and would just like to hibernate for the day, but as this is not a likely outcome, what should we do about it?

The temptation at this point is to look for a reason or meaning in your misery, but this would be a complete waste of time and only serve to make a bad situation a whole lot worse. Think about this logically. If you knew the reason and what it meant, then you could do something about it. But you don't.

I like to put my money where my mouth is, so I wrote this chapter in the midst of my own "pissed off for no reason day", which shall henceforth be known as a POFNR day.

Am I bored? I don't know. Am I angry at someone or something? I don't know. Am I feeling sorry for myself? I don't know, and I don't care. It is what it is, and I know from experience it will resist every attempt at self-analysis and make me feel worse. There doesn't have to be a reason, it doesn't have to mean something. X does not have to equal Y; sometimes X is just X, period.

At this point if you haven't thrown the book at the wall or pulled the pages out with your teeth, you might be interested to learn a new way of dealing with your POFNR days. Okay, so what should you do? *Do nothing* is the simple answer. That's it—there is no more. (Now you can throw the book at the wall.)

There is value in just doing nothing, but probably not in the way you think. Change the habits of a lifetime, and instead of trying to make X=Y, just let X be X for a change.

So what? You are pissed for no apparent reason. Big deal. Don't make it worse than it already is by looking for answers your mind can't supply. It will only serve to compound your misery.

> **Be an observer of your emotions, not a referee.**

Take a step back from the battle and say to yourself, "Yes, I'm fed up", "Yes, I'm bored", "Yes I could do without this", and then say, "But guess what: it is what it is, and it shall pass without any interference from me."

Your internal voice can be quieted by simply accepting, for now, that things are the way they are. Don't fight it; this isn't going to last forever. Think of it as a process you have to go through which requires no input on your part.

If you do this thinking process and keep doing it on your POFNR day, I can guarantee it will give up its grip on you a lot sooner than it would have if you had struggled against it. Let the mood flow around you and over you and don't interfere. You are more than your thoughts.

Remember, the subconscious mind learns by repetition, and you have taught it to feel a certain way and to react in a certain way when you have "one of those days". Maybe it's time to teach it a new way.

Imagine how useful it will be in the future to have a strategy ready when you feel one of those days coming on.

Also, remember the subconscious mind is slippery and will try and return you to previously learned behaviour. Be aware and recognise, if you are thinking words like "What if?" or "Why me?" or "I should be this or that?", this is just your inner critic trying to restore balance. Persist with not persisting, and it will soon get the message.

To apply the process you've just learned, you will have to wait until you have a POFNR day of your very own. If you are anything like the rest of us mortals, you won't have to wait very long.

Anyhow, to sum up, here's what to do. Or rather, not do:

- Don't analyse.
- Don't ask, "Why me?"
- Don't look for a reason.
- Don't manufacture an explanation.
- Don't attach meaning to something that has no meaning.
- Don't get into a two-way conversation with yourself.
- Don't get involved; be an observer, not a referee.

CHAPTER 22

Mind Your Language, You Loser

I looked forward to writing this chapter as it gave me a chance to insult everybody while pretending to help. Just joking, although what follows is really no laughing matter. Everyday language is something we don't give much thought to. I would like to share with you why I think it deserves some thought. Get ready to be insulted.

You are a loser. You are also a moron, an idiot, and you never get anything right.

I didn't think you would mind me calling you those things as you are probably calling yourself a lot worse every day of the week. How easy it is to berate ourselves for no apparent reason. We are so used to using negative terminology about ourselves that if I asked you why you do it, you would probably say, "It's just a figure of speech."

I have news for you. It isn't a figure of speech. It's an identity statement about yourself, and it's causing you untold harm.

Let's back up a bit, and it will all become clearer. Picture the scene (I really want you to imagine this happening): You are walking down the street and you see me in the distance walking toward you. As we get closer, you hear me muttering something, but can't quite make out what I am saying. So you say, "Excuse me, I can't hear what you're saying". I answer, "Oh, I was just saying what a loser you are, and you also look like a moron."

How does it feel when you imagine this scenario? Could you feel anger starting to rise? Maybe you feel rejection, or maybe I made you feel like something stuck to the bottom of my shoe. Would you let me off with calling you those names, or would I deservedly wake up in hospital with a surgical team staring down at me as they attempt to remove your fist from inside my face?

That's interesting, don't you think? You don't mind calling yourself these derogatory names, you just don't want someone else doing it. The bad news, is it doesn't matter if someone else calls you these names or you say them to yourself. The effect it has on your neurology is exactly the same.

There is a part of your mind called the subconscious which takes things very literally; it also learns by repetition. Can you see where this is going? If you are berating yourself with what you think is only a figure of speech, it has exactly the same effect as if I am saying the words to you in all seriousness. But it doesn't end there. The subconscious mind will produce a feeling to match what you are thinking; it's just doing what it does.

Think of it like this. If I were to say, "You have a big nose" twice a day to you for the next week, by the end of the week you will be looking into the mirror checking out your nose to see if it's true. But hey, it's just a figure of speech, it doesn't matter … right?

So why does it matter? It matters because every single time you make a negative statement about yourself, the statement starts to become part of your identity. It starts to become part of you.

Let's say, for argument's sake, your poison of choice is the statement, "You are so stupid. You never get anything right." What effect will this have? Actually, I will answer the question with another question—how many people do you know who constantly refer to themselves as stupid actually act stupid? You know the ones. They're always saying, "I can't apply for that job—I'm too stupid," or "I couldn't do that—I'm too stupid," or "I can't ask her out on a date—she's too intelligent for me".

Give a dog a bad name, and you have a bad dog … so goes the saying. Is this really what you want for yourself? Do you constantly want to think of yourself as lacking? But it's only a figure of speech … right?

And here's another news flash: subtle put-down statements are just as powerful as overt ones. Let me give you an example from my own life, that turned into a self-fulfilling prophecy. If I ever felt an episode of depression coming on, I used to say, "Damn (or words to that effect), I'm going to be depressed for the next three days". And yes, you guessed it, that's exactly what happened. For the next three days, I was down and depressed. I would then come out of it after approximately three days. This went on for quite some time until the penny finally dropped.

I am happy to say I would *never* dream of saying something like this now. I recognise the self-inflicted harm I would be causing. It's all too easy to let something we are saying to ourselves on a regular basis just slip by unnoticed. It becomes part of us, and before we know it, we are living it.

I will give you another example from a client I worked with. Her favourite saying was "I can't make decisions". This lady was morbidly obese; her self-imposed affirmation was causing untold damage because naturally she couldn't decide to eat healthily. Can you see the connection?

Another example: I heard someone say, "I love smoking." How dangerous is it to link the word "love" with something so lethal? What do you think the chances would be if—this person ever tried to quit smoking—of their actually being able to stop?

Will refraining from saying these statements help you lose weight and stop smoking? No, that will require a lot of hard work on your part, but why not tip the balance in your favour?

If you are making a negative statement about yourself on a regular basis, then it is time to play detective. What started or triggered you into saying this statement? Let me give you an example. The lady who said, "I can't make decisions" was amazed to find out that making decisions wasn't the problem. Taking responsibility for the consequences which flowed from those decisions was the real problem.

Don't take the detective bit too seriously, as it really doesn't matter *why* you are making the statement. The only thing which *really* matters is you *stop* doing it. If you are determined to be Sherlock Holmes, you might find the chapter "The Awareness Solution Technique" of benefit. So the next time you are getting ready to berate yourself or make a negative statement which starts with the word "I", think twice. Otherwise, you might get what you wish for.

There are two equally effective ways to remove a damaging statement from your vocabulary:

- Ask someone who knows you well, and who will give you an honest answer, to tell you what statements you make about yourself on a regular basis (such as "I can't make decisions"). Don't be surprised if something unexpected comes up. Now you have a starting point. Look and listen for the phrase in your everyday speech, and then systematically remove it. It will take a little while to do this, but the results will far outweigh the effort. If you say the phrase by accident, follow instantly by saying, "That's not true," or "I didn't mean to say that," quietly to yourself. A fuller description of how to do this can be found in the chapter "I Should, You Should".

- The second way to remove a negative statement from your vocabulary is to listen to your own language very carefully. Write down on a piece of paper the statements you think are causing you the most damage. Count how many times in a day you are making the statement, and write the numbers down. There is nothing like seeing it in black and white, as you then can't deny that it's happening. Just like before, systematically remove the statement from your vocabulary.

One thing you will certainly start to notice when you remove negative statements from your vocabulary is how much other people make negative statements about themselves. It seems we have conditioned ourselves to accept negativity as being normal. It's just not true; making negative statements is just another learned behaviour. As such, with a bit of effort, it can just as easily be unlearned.

I don't know if you've ever heard the saying, "Change your thoughts, and change your life." Well, the words you speak to yourself are just an internal expression of what you are thinking. So how about changing those thoughts to something that would be of benefit, instead of undermining yourself? Consider changing your inner dialogue with the process I have shared with you. It might change *your* life, too.

CHAPTER 23

Confidence Is Simple, Not Easy

Picture the scene. I am getting out of the car that drove me to the building I most dreaded visiting for the last six months. It looks exactly like I thought it would, dark and unwelcoming. As the car pulls away, I look over my shoulder wishing I was still inside that car going anywhere—anywhere but here.

I walk slowly up to the building, wondering what awaits me once inside. How many people will be there? Will they like me? Will they even talk to me? Up those long winding steps I go until I reach it … the room of terror, Room 126. I open the door and shuffle quietly toward my seat, hoping no one notices me. But of course they do, and we exchange nervous smiles.

I sit down on a chair which forms part of a semi-circle facing the teacher. Nowhere to hide. We are all looking anxiously at each other, each wondering why we came here, each wishing we could be somewhere else. Finally the teacher arrives, and he just seems to fill the room with his presence. He starts speaking those words everyone dreads to hear: "State your name, and tell us a little about yourself." Thankfully he starts with the person furthest away from me.

I have one eye on the teacher and one eye on the door. I want the floor to open up and swallow me whole. I'm starting to feel a bit nauseous and hot. One more person to go, and then it's me. Finally, the teacher fixes me with a gaze that leaves me in no doubt that it's my turn to speak. I open my mouth and start talking so fast I feel as if I've been taken over by an unseen force. I can hardly remember my own name. I am fast running out of something to say, and then ...

At last my ordeal is over, and the person next to me is starting into their own little speech. My heartbeat starts to slow down, and I feel nearly human again. Finally I've made it through—the first hour of my first day at school ... except that it wasn't. What I just described was my first day of training to become a therapist. I might have looked like an adult, but I felt like a five-year-old. Why? Because my brain had been hijacked by its own internal defence mechanism. I had exposed myself to a new and challenging situation, and my brain was preparing my body to run away by flooding my system with adrenaline, which then turned me into something resembling a jabbering idiot.

Today I would quite happily sit and teach that same class without so much as a deep breath. So what changed? I gradually and deliberately exposed myself to ever more challenging situations until I acquired the confidence I desired. That's how gaining self-confidence works. We don't come with an inbuilt confidence program; we have to work at it until it becomes second nature.

If I can do it, so can you. As a matter of fact if only one person can learn something, then anyone can learn the same thing. It just requires time and practice. Knowing you will possibly feel uncomfortable learning a new skill is the key to mastering that skill.

Knowing you will make mistakes lets you prepare for when they happen. That first-day-of-school feeling follows us all our lives. We just need a way of coping with it.

I have a little question which should get you thinking for a while. What are you good at? Think of the skills you have. Do you remember the first time you tried to practice a particular skill? It probably felt awkward; it probably seemed like it would be impossible to ever do correctly.

How did you become good at it? I can answer this for you: practice, practice, practice. You thought of your mistakes as just part of the learning process and didn't take them personally. And gradually, the skill seemed to become part of you. It was something that after a while required very little thought. You just did it.

If any of the above sounds familiar, then you already have a skill set that is easily transferable to obtaining self-confidence. There are more wrong assumptions made about self-confidence than possibly any other sought-after attribute.

People aren't born confident; it doesn't happen naturally. Confident people are not a special breed. Anyone (and I mean anyone) can be self-confident, but you have to want it badly enough. You have to expose yourself to socially challenging situations. It's like learning a new skill, it takes time and patience.

People believe they have to be confident *before* doing whatever scares them. The opposite is actually true; we need to do what challenges us in order to *gain* confidence. So if we are saying, "I would do xyz, if only I had more confidence," then we have effectively built ourselves a very nice little mind trap which will guarantee inaction.

We are waiting for a sign that we are now confident enough to do xyz. Only problem is the sign isn't going to show up. How do you know when you are confident enough? Does it come in a package marked "500ml of confidence, please use carefully"? Self-confidence is very subjective, it's how we feel about ourselves, not who we are.

Have a look at this sentence again: "I would do xyz, if only I had more confidence." There are two little words buried in the sentence that guarantee inaction and keep you from making any progress. The two words are "if only".

The words "if only" are filled with remorse and regret; they are firmly anchored in the past. They just sound all wrong. We are depending on hope and luck to get us through, rather than going out and obtaining something which, after all, is only a learned behaviour.

175

Let me put something straight right from the outset so there is no confusion: self-confidence is not arrogance. It is easy to view someone who is loud, larger than life, and who boasts about everything they do as being self-confident. In reality, they're just arrogant.

What most arrogant people don't want you to know, and will never admit, is their loudness and brashness has a lot to do with insecurity. They need the attention; they need you to notice them. They actually *lack* self-confidence, and are hoping lots of attention from lots of people will give it to them.

On the other hand, a self-confident person lets their actions speak for themselves. They have nothing to prove. They don't need to show the world how clever they are. They don't need to be the centre of the universe. You will know a self-confident person when you see one; they just have an aura of self-assuredness about them. They don't suffer the crushing feelings of not being good enough if they make a mistake.

If you lack self-confidence, I want to explain a little of what is probably going on in your mind. You will see you are not weak, just inexperienced.

We all have something called a comfort zone. This is actually a protection mechanism inside your subconscious mind. It gets activated when we try something new. It is there primarily to shield us from danger. Thousands of years ago it protected us from getting eaten by sabre-toothed tigers. It alerted us to changes in our environment and triggered a rush of adrenaline so we could either run away or fight.

We talked about this in another chapter, and if you have a good memory, you'll remember I said we still have this mechanism operating in us today. Although we are not at threat anymore from sabre-toothed tigers, the mechanism still gets activated whenever we step out of our comfort zone. As far as the mechanism is concerned, doing something out of the norm is dangerous. Okay, that's enough of the history lesson review. Let's continue.

So how does this all relate to self-confidence? Well, the good news is, we can lower the anxiety—the level of perceived danger—by practicing whatever it is we want to be confident doing. The bad news is you have to actually do the thing you really don't want to do. And you have to be prepared for the occasional slip-up. You are practicing a new skill, and it will take practice to get it right.

And here's another important tip. You have to forget about performing. You are not in a stage show, and no one is going to notice or care if you make a mistake. Even if you do make a mistake, the confidence police are not going to show up and give you a good beating.

Instead of focusing on your performance—on whether you're going to make a mistake and look bad—try focusing on what it is you came there to do. If it's public speaking, focus on the information you're trying to get across in your talk—not on whether the audience can tell if you're sweating or not. Get the focus off of you and on what you've come there to do.

Let me give you an example of how this change of focus can make a massive difference to your level of confidence. For the sake of our story, the character shall be known as "the nervous therapist". The therapist in question was newly qualified. Even the thought of seeing a real live person outside of the classroom terrified him (not a good thing if your speciality is treating anxiety).

Anyhow, the day came to see his first client and—you guessed it—he was sweating, shaking, and had palpitations. He managed to struggle through the first session unscathed. When the next client was about to arrive, he started sweating and shaking again. Something had to be done.

The nervous therapist sought help for the issue by going to see another therapist he knew well. The other therapist spotted the problem straightaway, as he himself had experienced the same difficulties when he first qualified. The problem with the nervous therapist was he was too concerned about his own performance. How he came across was of vital importance to him. He had to say the right thing at the right time, no mistakes. The client nearly became an irrelevance.

The solution was to concentrate totally on the client and to leave the need to look good at the door. No thinking about himself, only the client. This advice of the second therapist worked wonders. The sweating stopped, the nervousness receded, and the newly qualified therapist was able to get on with and enjoy the job of helping people. Can you see how being inside your own head all the time can have such a damaging effect?

So keeping our nervous therapist in mind, what is it you want to be confident doing? The more specific you can be the better. At this point think small steps, not huge leaps.

Let's say you want to be more confident talking to members of the opposite sex. The first thing you need to do is be able to practice in safety without fear of judgement, or without pushing yourself too far out of your comfort zone all in one go. A great place to practice is somewhere like a supermarket. No, I don't mean you go around talking to all the customers—that would probably get you arrested.

There are always staff members stocking shelves and cleaning. All you need to do is say something like, "The store is very busy today," or "Could you direct me to the xyz aisle?" Or use your imagination, as there are many similar things you could say. Then take it from there. The person might say something back to you, or you might just get a grunt. That's okay. You are here to practice, not look for a life partner.

You can also do the same with the cashier. As an added bonus, you also have a captive audience, as you will be there for at least two or three minutes. I'm giving you a supermarket just as an example. You can pick and choose wherever and whenever you want to practice. The important thing is not to worry how you are looking or coming across, as it doesn't matter. Just focus on the conversation.

> **No one is judging you half as harshly as you are judging yourself.**

Don't be surprised if you get a rush of adrenaline and maybe go a little bit dry in the mouth when you do this process. It's natural, it's normal, and it's to be expected. It's not a sign of weakness; it's a sign of inexperience. And how do you get experience? That's right—practice. And we can't get practice sitting at home, waiting for life to come to us. It's time for action, not thinking.

There is no magic formula to gaining confidence; it's simply a matter of practicing whatever it is you want to be confident doing. Initially, it's going to be a bit uncomfortable; there is no getting away from the fact. But the effort you put in will be more than rewarded.

After a while you will notice that what you thought was intimidating starts to become less intimidating. This is completely normal as your comfort zone has now expanded to take in your newfound skill. The important thing is to push your comfort zone at every opportunity until confidence is the new norm. I will leave it to you to come up with creative ways of meeting people; the good news is there are potentially seven billion people to practice on.

> **The great news is that once we become confident doing one thing, we can easily transfer the skill set to the next thing we want to do.**

If you really want to hone your skills and become confident talking to anyone, then I suggest buying some books on communication skills. It's not as intimidating as it sounds, and really comes down to being an effective listener. That's another skill which can be easily learned.

So what's it going to be? Are you waiting for confidence to show up in the post, or are you going to teach yourself a valuable life skill? It's up to you. I won't wish you luck, as you don't need it. All that's required is time, persistence, and a willingness not to give up at the first hurdle.

> **No matter how boring it gets, keep doing it. You are learning a new skill and just like a muscle, it needs to be exercised to become strong.**

What you think will influence what you do. If you're constantly telling yourself, "I don't want to do this," guess what? You won't do it. Your mind will always take the path of least resistance.

Force yourself to do what you don't want to do. Your mind is not going to give up its old habits without a struggle. It will constantly try and return to the old you. This is what it does.

It's not magic. It's just repetition, repetition, and a bit more repetition.

➢ **Get out there. Don't sit at home thinking about doing this. The mailman will not be delivering a packet of confidence tomorrow.**

CHAPTER 24

Be True to Yourself When You Can

Being true to yourself is about thinking your own thoughts and making your own choices in life. The unhappiest people I know are people who cannot be themselves. They are constantly on the alert to make sure they do not offend. Fitting in and going along with the pack is their one and only concern.

Let's have a look at a short list of situations we put up with, for the sake of fitting in:

- We go to social gatherings we don't want to go to.

- We put up with bad behaviour.

- We say yes, when we are aching to say no.

- We stay with partners we don't like.

- We spend money we don't have to impress others.

My particular favourite on the list is the last one, and it is something we see all the time but don't take any notice of. I can guarantee if you don't do this yourself, you know someone who does.

> **We spend money we don't have on things we don't need to impress people we don't like.**

Can you see the common link between everything on the list? The link is other people. We seem to have an inbuilt program that dictates our need to be people-pleasers, no matter the cost to us personally. Thousands of years ago, our survival depended on us being accepted by other members of our tribe. To be rejected meant certain death.

We still carry the same evolutionary program with us today; we still have the same need to be liked, the same need to fit in. The difference today is we are not going to face death if we don't. But what if you don't want to fit in, what then?

This is called being yourself, being authentic, and being unwilling to put up with someone else's ideas of what they think you *should* be.

What we fear most in the world is rejection. Did you know the same area of the brain is activated when we experience rejection as when we experience physical pain? Now you know why rejection hurts so much. We try so earnestly to avoid the pain of rejection that we're willing to put up with any amount of another kind of pain: denial.

Most of us, for the better part of our lives, deny the existence of the person *we* want to be. It is easier to smile and put on the mask of deception than risk the possibility of getting rejected. We have become experts in the art of putting up and shutting up.

We deny our relationship is going down the pan because it would mean having to face harsh reality. We deny the very existence of the little voice inside our head saying "I don't want to" and put it down to "just being silly".

> **The little voice is trying to tell you something, but you are not listening.**

Can we always be ourselves, all of the time? I am sure we could, but it wouldn't be a very happy existence. There are times when it is just not worth the hassle of standing on your principles. Sometimes, just sometimes, it is best to swallow hard and accept the situation. You don't have to like it; you just need to accept it.

There are no hard-and-fast rules—you have to do what you think is right when the occasion demands. The trick is knowing the difference between when it is right and when you are talking yourself into something out of a misplaced sense of obligation.

We only need to ask ourselves two questions to find out:

• Is this what I want?

• Is this good for me?

I can already hear you saying, "That would be selfish". If that's what you're thinking, then we are back to people-pleasing and needing to be liked again. If someone else is judging you as being selfish, then they think you should conform to *their* wishes based on *their* internal standards, not yours. Remember, I did say there are no hard-and-fast rules. You have to do what *you* think is right. Just make sure what you do is for the right reason.

There will always be times when you have to bend and go with the flow. It's part of being human. Being yourself is about accepting yourself as a human being, warts and all. Allow your humanity the full range of expression. Allow yourself the full range of emotions ranging from anger to serenity. Nobody is perfect or has a perfect life; it just looks like they might. We have no idea what goes on behind closed doors.

If you aspire to have the seemingly glorious lifestyle of a pop star or a Hollywood actress/actor, then ask yourself this: why do so many of them end up with depression, addicted to drugs or alcohol, or spend half their lives in rehab? Just like you and me, they are human. But unlike you and me, they have to spend their lives under the constant scrutiny of the media. Is this truly what you would like for yourself?

What can stop you from being you? Fear and only fear can stop you. Fear of what others might think, fear of rejection, fear of the unknown, fear of being different. That's okay—no one is expecting you to change the habits of a lifetime overnight. It's like building a wall; you do it one brick at a time.

It's okay to step back and see how far you have come now and again. Not everyone will like your wall; some people will even try to knock holes in it. It isn't personal, it's because they have walls all around them. They can't see any further than their own personal prison. Don't let anyone tell you what you can and cannot do, especially yourself.

If you remember, the title of this chapter is "Be True to Yourself When You Can". The "when you can" part is of special importance. Don't take on "being yourself" as your mission in life, otherwise you'll create your own prison. Being yourself doesn't mean you have to be perfect, because you are not perfect. If you try to be perfect, then you are not being yourself. Do the absolute best you can *whenever you can.* The rest will take care of itself. No one can ask more than that.

> ➢ **There is no one judging you more harshly than you are judging yourself.**

Think about the last sentence for a moment. Everyone on this planet, including you, is judging people and situations one hundred percent of the time. It is how we have evolved as a human race; it's how we gather information quickly. The curious thing is that we're making judgements of others constantly, but we don't want to be judged ourselves. When you put it like this, it sounds a bit ridiculous, doesn't it? How can we keep people from judging us?

The simple answer is, we can't. So doing something you don't want to do because of fear of judgement is a complete waste of time, as you're going to be judged anyhow. Judging is just what people do to each other.

We can't avoid it, no matter how much we might wish we could. If we try to avoid judgement by being people-pleasers, then other people are defining how we live our lives. And ironically, the people-pleasers get judged by those around them as "weak" because they are people-pleasers!

You see, there's no winning this game. You can't control what others think of you. You simply can't avoid being judged. What you can avoid is letting people's judgements control your life.

The hardest part is making the decision to change. We are hardwired by evolution to keep things the same. The fear you feel is not a sign of weakness, but a sign of your humanity. Being yourself is the highest expression of your humanity, and a sign you have truly evolved.

Being yourself whenever you can also requires a further step to be taken. It requires us to set boundaries. This entails learning how to say *no* and mean *no*. We will explore this important life skill next.

CHAPTER 25

'No'— A Short Sentence to Use Often

When I started writing this book, I never considered it might be hazardous to my health, but if my family ever read this chapter, I might be walking funny for a week or two. Here's the thing. I have been using the same techniques I am going to share with you for years on my family and friends. My secret will be out, and I won't be able to use the same methods ever again. I will have been rumbled ... damn.

I know what I will do: I will put it at the back of the book. Maybe that way they won't see it and I will be able to continue as before.

Anyhow, I want to share with you two ways of saying no without causing offence. The first method can be used on those occasions when no must be said emphatically and plainly. It can come across as being a bit blunt, so use it sparingly.

The second method is a lot more subtle, and can be easily altered to suit any situation. I call it "saying no without saying no". I used this method quite recently with my own relatives. Now can you understand why it is at the back of the book?

Of all the things I have shared with you, the ability to say no has got to be one of the most important. Being able to say no affects every part of your life: work, relationships, setting boundaries, you name it. If you want to be yourself whenever you can, then the setting of boundaries is a skill you need to acquire. Saying no and meaning it is the quickest way to do this.

Such a small word, yet extremely difficult to say. Why is it so?

It's difficult because you have to make a choice, and this choice can potentially mean rejection. We already know how much rejection hurts, but who are you really hurting when you say yes but want to say no? You are hurting yourself.

People-pleasers are rarely happy. They give little bits of themselves away until there is nothing left to give. I once heard a people-pleaser say, "Life is like living in a prison. I close the door and take off the fake mask, and I am left with nothing".

Did she do anything about her problem? She did not. Nothing was done because she didn't want to "let people down". She lived in fear of rejection. It didn't seem to matter if the exact same people were letting *her* down. Unfortunately, to be a people-pleaser, you also have to assume the role of victim.

Saying no can feel a bit uncomfortable despite what all the assertiveness books would have you believe. We are breaking social norms; we are doing something that is not expected from us. We're going against a lifetime of training by our parents and teachers who expected us to "be nice" and "not offend" and "not step out of line".

There is one important rule you must adhere to if you want to make saying no as pain-free as possible. You never get pressed into justifying your reasons for saying it. Don't worry— I am about to explain how to do it. I will give an example in a moment.

But understand this: if you justify your reason for saying no, the person doing the asking will come up with another reason for why you should say yes. Here's a step-by-step guide to getting it wrong. I am going to call our victim June, for no other reason than that was the first name which popped into my head.

- Hello, June. Do you want to meet for lunch?

  I can't. I'm busy at work.

- You are always so busy. Everyone deserves a break.

  I just can't get away from my desk.

- It will only take thirty minutes.

This scenario will continue until June gives in, because it's easier for her to just go with the flow, even if she doesn't want to, than to argue every objection the other person throws at her.

Now a step-by-step guide to getting it right:

- Hello, June. Do you want to meet for lunch?

  No, I can't, but thank you for asking.

- Are you busy?

  No, I just can't go today. Maybe tomorrow.

- Okay, I'll see you tomorrow.

Can you see the difference between the two scenarios? In scenario one, June's friend is feigning sympathy to get her own way. In scenario two, June is being polite—there is no rudeness—but she doesn't let herself get pressured into justifying her answer. She doesn't owe it to the other person to give her reasons for saying no, which would just invite debate about her decision. She merely needs to inform the other person of her decision.

It also helps to sweeten that word with "but thank you for asking". "No, but thank you for asking" works wonders in most situations. You might find a few seconds of silence to be very effective just after saying the word "no", as the silence gives added emphasis and power to your answer.

Nine times out of then, this will be the end of it. But what if the other person counters with, "Why not?"

Here's what you answer with: "Because I don't want to," or "Because I can't."

If you can avoid it, never give details of the reason for your no. If you do explain the details, the other person is back in control, and your opinion—your decision—is rendered invalid. Make every effort not to answer with a specific reason, as that invites the argument to begin.

There are thousands of different situations when you can say no without appearing aggressive or rude. It will be up to you to find out when no is appropriate. Saying no is about getting other people to respect your boundaries. If someone cannot take no for an answer, they are saying your opinion—indeed, your freedom of choice—doesn't count.

When it comes right down to it, there are really only two situations when a person should say no:

- When you can't do something

- When you don't want to do something

Well, that's the first technique. You use it when you must speak very plainly, when you expect the other person won't take the hint if you answer subtly. The second technique, which I'm about to describe, is for use when you can say no without using the actual word—when you think you can gently decline without there being a fight. As with the first technique, this second one can initially feel uncomfortable, but you have my promise it gets easier with practice.

I can't believe I'm going to tell you about this next technique considering how much trouble I will get into with my own family. Can I come and live with you if it all goes wrong?

My extended family was putting pressure on me to attend an event I didn't want to go to. I just couldn't think of a way of getting out of this event without offending anyone. My family was using every tactic under the sun to force me to attend. Guilt, sympathy, veiled threats, you name it. Anyhow, I came up with a plan to completely alleviate the situation, and at the same time not offend. The shortened conversation with my family went as follows:

- Are you coming to the event? Everybody is going to be there.

   I'm sorry. I can't go. (silence)

- Why not?

   Thank you for asking, but unfortunately I can't afford to go (silence).

- Oh, okay then. Maybe next year.

Can you see what happened here? I first acknowledged the request ("Thank you for asking") and then stated a reason for not going ("I can't afford to"). Now I know I just told you never to give them your reason, but this is an exception to general advice.

Why? Because no one is going to ask, "Why can you not afford it?" That would break a social norm. It's just not done. Nor are they likely to say, "That's okay. I'll pay your way myself," as few people are *that* generous.

Bottom line: saying "I can't afford to" is a great way to say no, without having to actually use the 'no" word, and at the same time get people to politely accept your answer. I know ... sneaky, isn't it?

I knew full well my relatives were not going to pay a thousand dollars to get me to that event. Sometimes that's what it takes to make sure your boundaries are respected. I'm quite sure you can up with a hundred variations of the examples I have shared with you. The important thing you have to remember is:

> **Never let them pressure you to justify your reason for saying no.**

Have a bit of fun with this. No need to get nasty by saying no at every possible opportunity, but practice until it becomes a skill that doesn't make you feel uncomfortable. Once you have mastered it, you'll come to realise just how important a skill it is. Maybe you could even pass it on to someone else.

Imagine if kids were taught in schools how to say no effectively. Sounds like a great idea for another book. Only problem is, I probably won't be alive to write it, if this book gets into the wrong hands.

CHAPTER 26

Final Thoughts

What do you mean there are no more biscuits? After all we have been through? That's it, I'm going home. No, I don't want a cup of coffee instead.

Wow … what a journey. I trust you enjoyed the ride and obtained something of practical value for yourself. When I finally arrived at writing the conclusion to my book, I thought I could end with some sort of motivational speech, the same as I have seen in countless other self-help books. Instead, I am going to do what I have endeavoured to do through the rest of the book, which is to speak honestly.

When I first decided to write this book it seemed like such a simple idea: write all my ideas down, and presto—a book is born. I couldn't have been more wrong, as when I started writing my own inner critic decided to come out to play. Most chapters were a struggle, which is what I expected because I had to keep referring to events which happened to me personally. How did I cope? By using the exact same strategies I shared with you.

We are all a work in progress, myself included. I had to hack my way through my own tangled mess with the mind machete I was going to lend to you. Then I realised I need it for my own continuing journey. The fact is, you have a mind machete of your own. It's just a bit rusty from lack of use. Using the techniques I have shared with you, it won't be long until it is sharp again.

If you were to ask me for one piece of advice to ensure your success (however you define it), it would probably be the complete opposite of the advice I have read. I would never advise you to "just go for it" as this would assume by just reading this book you have been imbued with some sort of special power. It would also assume I thought you were broken and I fixed you. It's just not so.

My advice would be to pick a chapter that resonated with you and practice the techniques until they become your own. Then repeat the process with the other chapters until they become second nature.

> **Take small steps on your personal road to courage.**

This is exactly what I did on my road. If it worked for me, it will work for you. If one person can do it, anyone can do it. Making peace with your inner critic is the greatest gift you can give yourself. Just take the first step, it could change your life.

NOTES

NOTES

_____
_____
_____
_____
_____
_____
_____
_____
_____
_____
_____
_____
_____
_____
_____
_____
_____
_____
_____
_____
_____
_____
_____
_____
_____

NOTES

Made in the USA
Middletown, DE
16 August 2023

36853988R00116